"For Christians who are struggling to reconcile their call to faithfulness and a desire to achieve financial freedom, this book is a must-read. Skillfully blending heartfelt personal testimonies, thought-provoking interviews, and deep biblical insights, it offers a balanced and transformative perspective on wealth creation. The authors beautifully illuminate how financial stewardship can align with God's purpose, encouraging readers to pursue success without compromising their faith. This inspiring work is a beacon of hope and wisdom for believers navigating this vital tension."

Matthew L. Watley, Senior Pastor,
Kingdom Fellowship AME Church

"*How to Get Rich Without Going Spiritually Broke* will transform the way Christians think about money and wealth building for the good of themselves and their neighbors."

Ekemini Uwan, Public Theologian
and co-host of Truth's Table Podcast

In "*How to Get Rich Without Going Spiritually Broke*," Lewis and Denton remind us of God's boundless generosity and inspire us to embrace His willingness to help us succeed. With biblical principles at its core, this book powerfully asserts that we must believe in our ability to succeed and transform our circumstances, recognizing that we were designed for accomplishment.

Keyana Russ, CFP®, RICP®

"You can love God AND desire wealth! This book is a game changer for Christians who were raised believing wealth and holiness are at odds. With candor, the authors tell how messages around money and spirituality either have been nonexistent, negative, or misinterpreted. Here is the book that breaks the silence and gently unravels many of the threatening and faulty teachings about wealth. Readers will come away not only with healthy new attitudes around acquiring wealth from experts, but they will also learn how to apply the biblical principles that support Christians living comfortably, setting up future generations, and sharing generously."

Cynthia T. Turner Wood, Senior Pastor,
Dayspring Community Church

HOW TO GET RICH
WITHOUT GOING SPIRITUALLY BROKE

7 Lessons for Money and Life

CASSANDRA LEWIS & FANIA DENTON

Cover design and interior formatting by KUHN Design Group | kuhndesigngroup.com

Author Picture: Norma Molina

How to Get Rich Without Going Spiritually Broke
Copyright © 2025 by Cassandra Lewis and Fania Denton
Published in Lanham, Maryland by Lewis & Denton

For more information, visit: https://wealthyandrighteous.com

ISBN 979-8-9924632-0-0 (paperback)
ISBN 979-8-9924632-1-7 (ebook)

Library of Congress Cataloging-in-Publication number: 2025903247

To our mothers. Those who birthed us and those who carried us forward with love.

CONTENTS

Preface 9

Introduction 17

Be Attitudes 21

1. Be Right-Minded 23

2. Be a Good Steward 43

3. Be Spirit-Led 59

4. Be Bold 75

5. Be Intentional 95

6. Be Diligent 109

7. Be Generous 127

Conclusion 143

Scripture Index 147

Notes 149

Acknowledgments 151

About the Authors 153

PREFACE

Our journey to write this book began with a phone call to catch up on each other's lives. It was the latter part of 2017, and as the new year loomed, we were both eager to get a jump start on sharing plans of how we would do things differently in the coming year. When we had spoken a few months earlier, we lived in two different states and chatted away about a women's conference we would launch together. Those plans didn't pan out, but our enthusiasm about planning a women's event was not dimmed.

Now, after Fania's relocation, living mere miles from each other, we regarded the coming year as a turning point—the one in which our dreams would be finally realized. Cassandra had even written up her plan for "30 days to a new life in 10 steps!" dated December 1, 2017. She regarded the list as a thing of beauty. It touched on the important areas of her life—faith, family, career, and health. It seemed that everything was covered. The year 2018 would be one of walking in divine purpose and fulfillment!

We spoke with the ease of friends who have not only known each other for over thirty years, but also have similar backgrounds. We're both immigrants—Cassandra was born in Grenada and Fania in Belize. We're both elder daughters of women from whom we've learned valuable lessons about hard work, resilience, and sacrifice, among other things. After four years of friendship forged in high school, we separated for college, obtained advanced degrees, and worked hard in our respective fields: higher education for Cassandra and law for Fania. The dedication and long hours paid off in many ways, such as promotions, the respect of our colleagues and managers, and the ability to contribute to comfortable lifestyles for ourselves and our families.

Still, despite a measure of success, over the years we've both wondered if what we have achieved is all there was for us. At times, we've found ourselves wanting to spend more energy on the things we are truly passionate about. These things—like academic enrichment programs for under-resourced children, seminars and workshops for women, ministry opportunities in our local church, advocacy on behalf of indigent populations, and philanthropic work in our native countries—receive only a small portion of our time and attention because of demanding work schedules. These are the kinds of activities that truly matter to us yet were relegated to our spare time. When we lived in different cities, in between catching up on life, reminiscing about high school, and discussing the changing demographics of the Brooklyn neighborhoods where we grew up, we'd spend hours sharing one idea after the other. During these conversations, our ideas took flight, energized by the enthusiasm and imagination of kindred spirits, only to come down to earth like neglected and deflated balloons when we said our goodbyes.

For some reason, our call on that particular evening in late 2017 took a different turn. Perhaps it was a recognition of our recurring cycle of unfulfilled dreams that unexpectedly interrupted our usual catching up session and led to some serious truth-telling, or rather, truth-asking. "So, what is it then? After all these years of dreaming, strategizing, and making plans, why has nothing changed? What will it take for us to really live the lives of abundance marked by fulfilling work, financial freedom, and philanthropy that we've been speaking about for years?" We cannot remember who actually asked the questions. Maybe we both thought about them at the same time.

Our call that night ended, but the questions persisted. As time went on, the questions burned with renewed urgency and dominated our conversations. How can we pursue what we believe to be our true purpose, yet be able to support our families, enjoy life, and give to the causes we hold dear? Equally important, how do we do so in a way that is consistent with our faith? As committed Christians, however we pursued financial freedom had to be consistent with our convictions about God. After years of wishful thinking, it was clear we didn't have the answers. So, we committed to praying and seeking an answer from God. Then one day the Lord answered, not with the details we were looking for, but with one simple instruction: go and ask those who have done it—those who have achieved financial success, while prioritizing their Christian faith.

This book is the fruit of our questioning and that instruction from the Lord. It is born out of our desire to acquire, put into practice, and share actionable knowledge of how wealth is amassed, sustained, and perpetuated by people of faith. Wealth is not the primary subject of this book. God is. Moses said in Deuteronomy 8:18, "And you shall remember the Lord your God, for it is He who gives you power to get wealth." As far as we are concerned, anybody can become wealthy. We wanted to know how to do it while honoring God. This book is not a get-rich-quick scheme or a formula for growing millionaires.

It is rooted in our belief that the Bible is the ultimate source of wisdom, including wisdom on wealth building and financial freedom.

Along the journey of writing this book, we looked at our own lives—our upbringings, our belief systems, and our patterns of behavior. Despite our accomplishments, and the overall feeling of having come far from very humble beginnings, we recognized there was still something amiss. Something we couldn't put our fingers on was holding us back from experiencing the level of success and fulfillment we believed God had intended and equipped us to achieve.

Sometimes answers do not come quickly. Instead of 2018 being a year of realizing the goals we had imagined the year before, it marked the beginning of what became a more than seven-year journey filled with discovery, learning, and growth. It took seven years to finish writing this book. It hasn't been easy. Growth seldom is. Countless hours have been spent together discussing what we learned and encouraging, challenging, and praying with and for each other. By far the hardest aspect of this journey has been the personal, internal work of self-interrogation and deep reflection that was necessary to understand the habits and financial decision-making that kept us stuck, doubtful, frustrated, unfulfilled, financially burdened, and living far below our potential.

Some of our introspective work was done with the guidance of expert coaches, spiritual guides, and wise friends. Much more was done alone, with and through the power of the Holy Spirit. As followers of Christ, we firmly believe that any conversation about our goals and objectives, even as they relate to finances, has to be understood through the lens of God's view on the subject. We believe God is the expert on every subject, so before we interviewed one person or began reading any books about wealth building, we started first with the Bible.

While we understand the value of the leading financial publications on which many people rely, we would not neglect the rich source of wisdom that is the Bible. God has a lot to say about money! By one count, there are over two thousand verses about financial stewardship in the Bible. God gives instructions on how to view money, how to get money, how to grow money, and what to do with money. The Lord did not leave us without guidance on such an important topic.

This book is unique. It is not simply a summary of what the Bible says about wealth, but it shares the thoughts, practices, and experiences of actual Christians who have put the principles of Scripture into action. These people have mastered how to get rich without going spiritually broke. If they could do it, so can we, and so can you. In soliciting their opinions, we formulated discussion questions designed to capture their beliefs and thought patterns, as well as their actual habits. We weren't just interested in what our interviewees thought, but we really wanted to know how they live.

This has been a personal journey for us from the very beginning. As Black women, we understand there are unique aspects of our backgrounds that impact both our outlook and access to capital. While we recognize a certain universality of principles of wealth creation across race and gender, we had to acknowledge the presence of real cultural obstacles to financial freedom for Black Americans. Some of these are historical. Others are contemporary. None of them are insurmountable. For these reasons, we chose to limit our interviews to wealthy Black Christians. We believe that also makes this book distinctive. It is rare to hear the voices of Black Christian wealth creators. Their perspectives are not important only to other Black Christians, but everyone can benefit from their wisdom and experience. We are excited to share it.

How did we find these people, you ask? At first, this seemed a daunting task. Did we know any millionaires? Would anyone we know admit to being a millionaire? After brainstorming about our own connections, reaching out to family and friends for referrals, and in one instance, boldly approaching a presenter at a conference, we came up with our final list. This list includes men and women from a range of careers and fields—from corporate executives to clergy to entrepreneurs. Most reside in the United States, but one is running a thriving business in Jamaica.

All of the interviews were conducted via telephone, except for one, which was held in person. In all but two cases, they were recorded and later transcribed, to ensure accuracy when recounting the information. When using direct quotations, we have gently edited the conversational flow of the interviews for the sake of readability.

Everyone with whom we spoke went above and beyond in answering our specific questions, and shared some personal details of their lives, including not only the triumphs but also the challenges. To honor the openness and level of sensitivity in which those we interviewed shared, particularly some who expressed even slight hesitancy in giving an open door to the intimate details of their families, we have chosen not to reveal their real names and have instead assigned each a pseudonym.

We've named one readily identifiable thought leader in the area of personal finance, award-winning journalist and *Washington Post* columnist Michelle Singletary. Her experience in this field, combined with the fact she is both a believer and a Black woman who is committed to educating and equipping the masses on money matters, made her an ideal person with whom to speak. We are grateful for her participation.

The experiences of the men and women we interviewed are by no means standard. Their backgrounds were as varied as the paths they took to achieve financial freedom. Some came from families that were already well-off and had parents who taught them about money, while others came from humble beginnings and had few, or no, "money mentors." For some, conversations about money began at an early age, and they were able to build upon a lifetime of shared wisdom and adapt it to their present lives. For others, the subject was never mentioned, except in the context of scarcity. These individuals shared stories of an early lack of knowledge and the resulting missteps as well as the process it took to restore them to financial health.

While the stories differed, there were many common themes that ran throughout our discussions. We have sought to summarize these themes and to present them in a way that anyone can implement in their life, no matter where they are on their financial journey. Along with these stories and themes, we share snippets from our own lives, both good and bad. Finally, interwoven among it all, there are lessons from the Bible that we believe are instructive on the topics at issue.

A word about faith and finances. Unfortunately, money has sometimes been a sore spot in the church, especially when speaking about wealth creation. There are segments of the Christian community that frown upon the idea. We grew up in very loving congregations, but at the same time, we recognize that our early foundation in a very conservative Christian tradition instilled within us some beliefs and behaviors that have made it more difficult for us to have healthy relationships with money. We honor our pasts but are convinced today that there is a better way. We believe firmly that "the love of money is a root of all kinds of evil" (1 Timothy 6:10). We believe everything should be put in its proper place: under God. Like anything else, money, at its best, is a tool the Lord has provided to glorify Him and bless His people. Perhaps this book can help you wrestle through some of these same issues and questions we struggled with, as we made peace with the idea of wealth creation.

INTRODUCTION

Being rich or wealthy means different things to different people. The classic definition is generally limited to an accumulation of money or financial resources, but many people include in their definition an overall state of health, wellness, and abundance in other areas of life. While we find value in these expanded definitions, in this book, references to being rich or wealthy will focus on the state of our financial affairs. We are defining *wealth* or *being rich* as having an abundance of financial resources. For us, being wealthy would enable us to do things like buying a home in cash, paying up front for our children's education, without them having to worry about student loans, and giving generously to people and causes we hold dear. It would also mean not having to work a particular job out of financial necessity and leaving a financial legacy for future generations.

In the chapters that follow, we will share the advice of the millionaires we interviewed, as well as our own stories, under a framework we call the *Be Attitudes*. Inspired by the two-part format of the original Beatitudes found in the Sermon on the Mount (see Matthew 5), our *Be Attitudes* is presented as a condition and a promise. The first part of each *Be Attitude* represents one of seven different ways of being, or attitudes, found prominently in the wealthy Christians we interviewed. The second part offers the promise that, as a general principle, resulted from their faithfulness to the first part.

This format, just as it does in Jesus's teachings in Matthew 5, underscores the principle that there is a proper action leading to a desired result. This theme is central to wealth building. As we will see, becoming wealthy is not achieved by just hoping and wishing, approaching our finances haphazardly, or engaging in fly-by-night schemes. Furthermore, for Christians, wealth building involves more than just an act of our will. It starts and ends with the Father—having a right understanding of Him, seeking Him throughout the journey, and honoring Him in our financial decisions, as well as our relationships with others.

Although each chapter describes a separate *Be Attitude,* and each is given due treatment, they are by no means independent of each other. Many of the concepts are interrelated and must be applied in concert with others. For example, the first three *Be Attitudes, Be Right-Minded, Be a Good Steward,* and *Be Spirit-Led,* are all-encompassing. They are foundational. In practicing any of the other *Be Attitudes,* it's important to have the right mindset, to properly manage what you've been given, and to be led by the Spirit of God. To emphasize this, we frequently refer to these three chapters when making a point in the later ones. In addition, they are in essence God-focused. Each one relates to how we view and interact with the Father, and to how this view reflects on, and influences our relationship with, money.

The next three *Be Attitudes, Be Bold, Be Intentional,* and *Be Diligent,* focus more on actions we must take in order to build wealth. These chapters comprise what can perhaps be considered the practical steps to take—the ones most likely to be found in the leading how-to books. Perhaps the ones that as spiritual people we least want to hear, much less practice. Being bold, intentional, and diligent speak of moving beyond our comfort zones, engaging in the process, and persistent hard work. These are dirty words for those conditioned to think that God will just hand everything to us without any real action on our part.

Finally, *Be Generous* speaks to the element of wealth building that involves our relationship with others. We were created to be in relationship—first with God, then with each other. It is therefore not surprising that this topic featured prominently in our discussions.

Each chapter ends by summarizing major points, and by inviting further action from you, the reader, through sections called *Be Prayerful* and *Be Doers*. This is the space to do some reflective work about what you've just read and to identify areas where you may want to be proactive in your own life. We wrote this book together, but the internal work of processing each of the *Be Attitudes* is a deeply personal and individual journey. Take the time to do the physical and spiritual inventories. *Be Prayerful* is a way to approach the Father about the specific points that were discussed. Be still before God and allow Him to lead you. And finally, *Be Doers* is where you will name at least one step you can take, based on that chapter.

You may have picked up this book because you desire something different, something more. Maybe you feel burdened by the crushing weight of financial debt, overdue bills, and working impossible hours just to stay ahead. Perhaps you're just curious about our story and hopeful that you can pick up some new strategies to build on what's already working in your own life. Wherever you fall along that continuum, we urge you to read this book with an open mind and be receptive to change. If you are not satisfied with where you are financially or spiritually, we encourage you to evaluate your attitudes, habits, and priorities, as they relate to money, and to be brutally honest in this assessment. And finally, commit to change.

BE ATTITUDES

1. BE RIGHT-MINDED

Blessed are the right-minded, for they shall see the truth.

2. BE A GOOD STEWARD

Blessed are the good stewards, for they shall be rewarded with more.

3. BE SPIRIT-LED

Blessed are the Spirit-led, for they shall walk in God's will.

4. BE BOLD

Blessed are the bold, for they shall realize success beyond their dreams.

5. BE INTENTIONAL

Blessed are the intentional, for they shall accomplish their goals.

6. BE DILIGENT

Blessed are the diligent, for they shall enjoy the fruits of their labor.

7. BE GENEROUS

Blessed are the generous, for they shall prosper.

Chapter 1

BE RIGHT-MINDED

Blessed are the right-minded,
for they shall see the truth.

anging high above the altar of the church was a large, stiff banner, emblazoned with the words "Holiness Unto the Lord." It was the first thing you saw when you walked into the sanctuary. Its position and prominence made it clear that it was not there for show. The four words on the banner succinctly defined the theology and values of the church Cassandra and her mother attended soon after they immigrated from Grenada. When combined with the preaching, the banner's message overwhelmingly amplified God's holiness, to the exclusion of all His other character traits. The command to separate from worldly pleasures and sin in order to be acceptable to a holy God was a familiar theme that dominated church life. This church, built by Caribbean immigrants and tucked away between modest two-family row houses in Brooklyn, New York, has changed dramatically over the years. The impact of this early congregation, however, still endures.

Cassandra shared about her early faith experiences, as we worked through initial findings from our first round of interviews. Although our analysis was far from over, an emerging theme had our full attention. When it comes to wealth creation, what we think matters. What we think about money, certainly. But more importantly, what we think about God. As we wrestled with our own thoughts about wealth building, we were forced to consider the defining experiences that shaped our perceptions of both God and money.

"The church I grew up in was strict. I'm talking lots of no's: no pants, no makeup, no movies. Come out from among them! Be ye holy as I am holy," Cassandra shared, with a laugh, and her usual hint of theatrics. "No, but seriously it was a religiously conservative and charismatic church. We had a good time in church, and I loved the people, but to me, God was strict and a little scary. Perhaps there were other aspects of God that were emphasized, but I don't really remember them. The don'ts and no's dominated my perception," she admitted. "So, one of the challenges of that upbringing is that as a child, I formed a narrow view of God as a strict disciplinarian, an exacting figure of authority. This perception left little or no room for an image of God as a doting parent, ready and willing to lavish His affection on His beloved children."

Over the years, through much study, life experience, and soul-searching, Cassandra discovered the image of God developed in her childhood did not reflect His full character. While it is true He corrects and reproves us as part of His role as loving parent, He also demonstrates His love by blessing us richly from His bounty. And yes, that blessing is sometimes financial. We only have to look at the grandeur of creation to see that God is not stingy. There were times when God gave His people just enough for their daily needs, in order to emphasize their reliance on Him, like when He led the Israelites through the desert. But there were other times, like when His children finally possessed the promised land, when He allowed His people to live in the overflow, enjoying resources that were above and beyond what they could wish for. Let's also not forget the wealthy saints of God we're introduced to in both the Old and New Testaments. Because Cassandra did not have this full understanding of God, she spent a large part of her early life focusing on His justice, to the exclusion of His goodness.

Fania's early experiences with getting to know the Lord were also formed through her attendance at church, albeit one with a different theological focus. She found the services to be mostly formal and regimental. The teachings were about a faraway Deity who did great things in the past and now looked down on humanity with a somewhat distant benevolence. As His children, there were certain rules we ought to follow, and the onus was on us to keep the lines of communication open through prayer—whether for the purpose of requesting needed help or thanksgiving, when it finally came. There was no emphasis on a living, close personal relationship with the Father; no guidance on seeking Him in all areas of your life, least of all about how to make and manage money.

Although our early religious experiences were different, they led us to a similar relational place with God. Some of His attributes were emphasized, some glossed over, and others completely left out. We saw Him through a distorted lens, and as a result, we did not have the right mindset about Him.

Our first *Be Attitude, Be Right-Minded*, underscores the most impactful lesson we have learned in our exploration of how to get rich without going spiritually broke. The lesson should not surprise you because we've all heard it before. It applies to just about everything in life, not just money. Here it is: mindset matters. We can't begin to discuss how to act with our money until we've discussed how to think about our money. In order to change our behavior, we must change our attitude. In this chapter, indeed throughout the book, we will discuss ways of changing attitudes that keep us broke, stuck, and unsatisfied! Adopting a right-minded perspective is essential for achieving wealth and fulfillment.

We believe there are three "right-minded" perspectives that are essential if you want to have a healthy relationship with money and wealth creation. First, you must have a right-minded perspective about God. Second, you must have a right-minded perspective about yourself. And third, you must have a right-minded perspective about money. The reality is, though, that sometimes embracing the right perspective is easier said than done. Sometimes it requires changing old habits and shedding entrenched, but unhealthy, attitudes of our past. On a very personal level, we discovered, over our time writing this book, that too many of our own attitudes and behaviors concerning money were rooted in misinformation, half-truths, or distortions. Our goal, then, is to challenge your perspectives and encourage more productive ways of thinking, where necessary.

TRUTHS ABOUT GOD

God Is the Owner of All the World's Riches

For the believer, any full understanding of money starts with acknowledging that all wealth, indeed everything, belongs to God (see Psalm 24:1). The Bible tells us that in the beginning, God created

The more we adopt a right-minded perspective that allows us to see the Father as generous, loving, and willing to bless us, the easier it will be to receive from Him.

the heavens and the earth (see Genesis 1:1). He doesn't turn ownership over to humanity but rather allows us to enjoy His creation.
In the first chapter of the book of Genesis, God told humans to be
fruitful and multiply, replenish the earth, and have dominion over
it (see Genesis 1:26–28). These and other verses reveal humankind's
relationship to the earth and its bounty as one of stewardship, not
ownership. We will explore our status as stewards more fully in the
next chapter, but it's necessary to mention here as it demonstrates
our position in relation to money and other things we consider as
our possessions.

God Is Good and Generous

Now, if God owns everything, how do we get the right to use
what He owns and how much of it can we use? As we noted above,
God commanded humans to be fruitful, multiply, and have dominion. The Father Himself has empowered us to use His resources.
Consider the parable of the talents in Matthew 25:14–30. According to the story, a man is going on a journey. Before he leaves, he
gives some money to three servants "in according to his own ability"
(v. 15). To one, he gives five talents (one talent was roughly equiv-
alent to twenty years' wages for the common worker), to another
two talents, and to the last, one talent. The first two servants both
take action and double the money they are given, but the servant
who was given one talent buries it in the ground. Upon learning
of their actions when he returns, the master praises the two who
increased their sums and promotes them. But for the third, who
buried his money, the master has a harsh rebuke. That sad fellow
watches as what he had is taken away and given to the one who
had earned the most!

The parable teaches us at least two very important principles. We will discuss the first principle here, and the second in chapter two. The first principle is that the master distributes varying amounts of talents to his servants as he sees fit. God is the ultimate decision-maker in how resources are distributed. We are all born into different families with different circumstances. Some people are born into privilege and have every financial advantage from the moment of birth, others are born into poverty and struggle all their lives, and numerous others fall somewhere in between. We don't have any control over where we fall on this continuum, but regardless of where we fall, the Lord's willingness to allow us access to His wealth and resources is evidence of His goodness and generosity. We have an obligation to be the best managers of what we've been given, and to take advantage of every opportunity life offers.

Most earthly parents take pride in providing well for their families, so why do so many of us have a hard time believing that the same is true about God? Do we think we are more generous and caring than He? Jesus stated emphatically, "If you then, being evil, know how to give good gifts to your children, how much more will your Father, who is in heaven, give good things to those who ask Him!" (Matthew 7:11). Again, these good gifts are not restricted to finances, but they certainly include them. The more we adopt a right-minded perspective that allows us to see the Father as generous, loving, and willing to bless us, the easier it will be to receive from Him. However, if we see Him as exacting and giving us only what we need and no more, we will be less likely to experience more of His generous nature. "Every good gift and every perfect gift is from above, and comes down from the Father of lights" (James 1:17).

TRUTHS ABOUT YOURSELF

You Are Capable of Building Wealth

Adopting a right-minded perspective about money and wealth building begins with our perceptions about God, but it doesn't end there. On our journey to financial wellness, we must not only have the right perspective concerning God, but we must also have the right perspective of ourselves. It's important we see ourselves as people who are capable of acquiring the right tools, or taking the necessary steps, to achieve our goals. In other words, we must believe we can succeed. We must believe we can change our financial situations for the better. We must have an unflappable right-minded perception of our own worth and potential. Of course, this understanding is tempered with knowing that ultimately it is God who gives us the ability to produce wealth (see Deuteronomy 8:18). Still, adopting the right perspective concerning how God might desire to open financial blessings to us is a struggle for many.

Like we shared about our perception of God, our view of ourselves and our ability to gain wealth was shaped by our early lives. Growing up in a small village in Belize, Fania's early experiences with money were not positive ones. It seemed as if everyone in her surrounding community was struggling to make ends meet. By the mid-'80s, neither electricity nor indoor plumbing had come to the part of the village where Fania lived. Homework and other tasks had to be done before dusk, or she would be sitting at the kitchen table, doing math by candlelight. If there was enough money that week, maybe there would be kerosene for the lamp.

For the most part, this subsistence living was the only life Fania knew—a cycle of constant struggle, lack, brief periods of ease, during which they enjoyed someone else's generosity, and the certain knowledge that, sooner rather than later, the lean times would return. This cycle was not strange to Fania, since everyone around her was struggling to get by. Everyone lived a day-to-day, hand-to-mouth existence. Even though Fania excelled in school and was encouraged by her family and teachers to keep studying hard, and to "make something of herself," she couldn't envision being wealthy. So limited was her view of her own potential, so small was her conception of success, she didn't even think a professional career was within her reach.

She could see herself getting a "regular" job and wearing a nice uniform to work. "I admired the female bank tellers who looked so sharp in their skirt suits," Fania noted, with a rueful shake of her head. "But anything else was beyond my frame of reference." It wasn't that Fania was never exposed to other professionals. Outside of her village, Belize City had its fair share of successful professionals and thriving, wealthy neighborhoods with all the modern conveniences. But the fleeting glimpses into this world did nothing to raise Fania's view of her ability to achieve on those levels. "They were not my kind of people. They didn't look like me. They didn't come from where I came from," Fania noted. "I had no idea how they achieved what they did. Forget about the wealth I saw on television shows. Those people existed on another planet."

One of the regrettable aspects of our formative years is that we didn't hear the message about achieving financial success from the church. Even though we attended church regularly, this part of the message of hope didn't reach our ears until much later on in our lives. For us, like it was, and probably still is, for many people, the topic of money, except in the context of its collection for various projects, or warnings about the danger it poses to our souls, was outside the purview of the church. Week after week, we were encouraged to look for a heavenly reward while daily needs went unmet and potential went unfulfilled. "To say this limited both my worldview and the view I had of my own capacity to break out of this cycle is an understatement," Fania shared.

When we interviewed Wayne, a best-selling author, motivational speaker, and media personality, he shared about his mission to break the types of limiting beliefs that keep Christians in financial bondage. Wayne has a roster of large corporate clients, has been featured on major news outlets, has his own XM Satellite Radio show, and leads an impactful ministry. He has written extensively on the theology of wealth, in which he seeks to dispel the idea that wealth and Christianity are somehow mutually exclusive. We were blown away by his message and his boundless energy. "You were designed for accomplishment. You were engineered for success, and you were endowed with the seeds of greatness. So, you must be willing and able to go out and make that greatness." With each one of these pronouncements, Wayne masterfully made his case for why more Christians, especially African American Christians, must shed the limiting, often shame-filled belief that money, and our ability to create wealth, are taboo subjects in the church. "God smiles on creating income, and even smiles on creating wealth...And it's not about the money," Wayne insists. "It's about the mission. We must be mission-minded, we must be mission-focused. We are here to be empowered to do something that makes a difference." Wayne's premise is that as people of faith, we are supposed to be high achievers in all things, including wealth creation. He proposes that wealth creation by believers is one of the systems by which God sustains the church and its work on earth. In other words, one of the primary reasons why Christians should create wealth is to pour back into others.

Genesis 1:27 tells us that we all, as human beings, were made in the image and likeness of God. He has made us all worthy to receive aspects of His personality and character. Part of His likeness is the ability to create and achieve. We think we can all agree that God is the ultimate achiever! There is nothing wrong with being high achievers. Once again, it's all about being right-minded. Achievement is not all about money, but as Wayne rightly asserts, it's a part of it. God reminds us in Deuteronomy 8:18 that He is in fact the One who gives us the power to produce wealth. Let's therefore get our confidence from Him and believe it when He says He takes pleasure in giving us good gifts (see Matthew 7:11).

You Are Deserving of Possessing Wealth

Wealth creation is not limited to a certain group of people, or to those from a specific background. No one person is more worthy than another. We may be limited by various factors, such as the circumstances of our birth, the knowledge we possess, or our own willingness to work toward this goal, but there is nothing inherent to one person that makes him or her more qualified to be wealthier than another. It is, therefore, not only important that we see ourselves as capable of building wealth, but also as deserving of possessing it.

After years of thinking to the contrary, adopting a right-minded view of self in relationship to money can be difficult. But it's not impossible. Brian's story modeled how to develop self-worth in our ability to be successful and turn our financial lives around. A native of Jamaica, Brian struggled financially and battled depression for many years because of the many personal setbacks in his life. He admits that, growing up, his family was poor, and at times he lived on the streets. Not surprisingly, he got in trouble with the law in his early teens. He summarizes his entire teenage years, during which he often had nowhere to sleep and nothing to eat, as "a time of suffering, pain, and heartache." The hardship continued into his adult years, as he lacked formal education, went through a divorce, and experienced estrangement from his church family. Lacking both the tools and the mindset for wealth building, Brian did not feel capable of achieving the basic necessities of life, much less attaining wealth.

His turnaround began as he delved into the Scriptures and daily asked the Holy Spirit for guidance. As he studied the Bible, he saw that his background didn't matter. What mattered was that he had a heart to follow after God and do His will. This right-minded conviction gave him the drive and motivation to persevere toward his goals. His journey hasn't been linear, nor without setbacks, yet today he operates one of the largest Christian television stations in the Caribbean and is able to enjoy the blessings of a complete turnaround in his life.

We said before that you must consider yourself deserving of the life you desire, including being wealthy. This is not the same thing as saying that because you are a Christian, God owes you a certain lifestyle or guarantees a life free from financial struggle. You are deserving because, as His child, He takes pleasure in blessing you and giving you good gifts. As a matter of fact, the Scriptures say He is good to all (see Psalm 145:9) and He sends the rain on the just and unjust alike (see Matthew 5:45). We are worthy because He has made us worthy, not because we have done anything to qualify ourselves. This is not the same as being entitled. As we saw in the parable of the talents we discussed earlier, the master gave a different amount to each person. He put no limit on their ability to multiply those talents, therefore the ultimate return was up to them. We should never forget that God is sovereign, and He gives gifts to all of us as He wills.

Do you believe you are deserving of the life you hope for? Do you believe you are able to create the life you desire? Do you believe you can be wealthy, or do you think you're always going to be just getting by, or struggling financially? Do you believe you have something valuable to offer in the marketplace for which you can receive suitable compensation? The way we answer these questions will greatly affect how far we go, financially. If lack has been the story of your family for generations, it can be very difficult to break free of the belief that deficit living is also your lot in life.

Many people with challenging financial stories in their background have accepted that lacking resources is just the way it's going to be for them. They view financial security as something only certain types of people can achieve. On the other hand, you may be part of a different group of people. Maybe you're not struggling. You enjoy a comfortable life. You can take your family on vacation once a year and give to your church. You even drive a nice car. But you're scared to risk pursuing abundant living because you tell yourself that maybe you should just be grateful for the life you have, for fear of losing it. That's what usually happens, right?

The people we interviewed charted the course for their own lives and believed they could achieve their goals. Not even the individuals who grew up in working-class households were constrained by what they experienced growing up. Instead, they credited their families or someone influential in their lives with instilling in them a belief in themselves, and in what was possible with God. Most admitted to a growing understanding of, and relationship with, money throughout their lives, but again, they became successful in building wealth in part because they believed that it was possible and that they could do it. Do you believe that the same is possible for you?

TRUTHS ABOUT MONEY

How we think about money determines how we relate to it. Notice we said *how* we think about money and not *whether* we think about it. That's because we *all* think about money. It is a consideration in just about every daily decision we make. Will we go to the movies tonight? What should we eat? Should we move out of the neighborhood? Should we go on vacation? All these questions have financial implications.

Wayne recalled that when he was young, "money was discussed in the church, but only in two ways: one, the church needs money, and two, money is the root of all evil." Wayne's experience is like that of many believers. How could something that's so necessary be not just evil, but the very root of evil? Of course, the verse in 1 Timothy 6:10 to which Wayne refers is misquoted. The text says, "For *the love* of money is a root of all kinds of evil, for which some have strayed from the faith in their greediness and pierced themselves through with many sorrows" (emphasis added). The verse cautions against the love of money, not money itself. It is a small omission that has a huge impact. It changes everything!

If we think money is evil, our attitudes toward it, and therefore our relationship with it, will be negative. But when we understand that the apostle Paul was cautioning against a depraved condition of the heart—the placement of money as an idol—we can ensure we are being right-minded and foster a healthy relationship with money.

One of the most popular biblical stories that has long poisoned the minds of believers against wealth creation is the story of the rich young ruler. In that story, a man approaches Jesus and asks Him, "Good Teacher, what good thing shall I do that I may have eternal life?" (Matthew 19:16). After suggesting to Jesus that he has been dutiful in living a righteous life, Jesus responds by saying, "If you want to be perfect, go, sell what you have and give to the poor, and you will have treasure in heaven" (v. 21). Many believe that surely, if Jesus instructed that young man to sell all his possessions and give the money to the poor, it must have been sinful for him to have so many possessions in the first place.

This story has many Christians thinking financial success in this world prevents one from going to heaven. Furthermore, if by chance one happens to get rich, he or she should give away all their money and worldly goods. Yet this thinking cannot be true. It is inconsistent with so many other passages of Scripture, and with the generous nature of God Himself. Consider these examples: Abraham was rich in livestock, silver, and gold. Isaac inherited considerable wealth from his father Abraham, yet his wealth continued to grow until he became very rich. Solomon was the richest king in the world, yet the rulers of other kingdoms brought him gifts of silver and gold (among other things) after visiting and hearing the wisdom that God had given him.

In case we think this was only an Old Testament phenomenon, Joanna and Susanna are named among the many wealthy women who supported Jesus's ministry. Joseph was a rich man of Arimathea who donated his own tomb to bury Jesus. And Lydia was a wealthy woman who supported the apostle Paul and started a house church. But the verses from 1 Timothy and Matthew, listed above, either misquoted or misapplied, have caused us to think negatively about wealth. Are there any others that readily come to mind for you?

Stories like that of the rich young ruler, which are often taken out of context, erroneously interpreted, or wrongly applied, are often, even if unintentionally, used to keep people in mental and financial bondage. This is especially true in the Black community. So many of us have held fast to these beliefs all our lives. They have informed our choices about careers, influenced our views of self and others, limited our pursuits, and ultimately shaped the very lives we've created for ourselves. In some Christian circles, there's a pride in poverty, as if poverty and piety go hand in hand. The less one has, the more holy he or she is. As we've seen with the wealthy individuals listed above, this is absolutely untrue. There are sinful poor people and there are righteous wealthy people. Being poor or struggling financially doesn't equate to righteousness.

There's a misconception that rich people think about money all the time—that they are obsessed with it—whereas those who are less well-off do not. Perhaps the thought is that without the worries associated with having money one can devote more of their attention to the things of God. Anyone who's ever truly been without money knows the error of that thinking. Those who are struggling to make ends meet, living from paycheck to paycheck, wondering how various bills will be paid, spend a great deal of time and energy thinking about money, maybe even to the point of obsession.

On the other hand, there are those who are financially secure who are free from this type of worry. Without question, a great deal of time and attention are necessary to formulate, implement, and cultivate a financial plan, but a lot of time and attention, not to mention angst, are also spent by those just getting by. The point is that there are poor people for whom money is an idol and there are wealthy people who have God first in their lives. It is all about having the right mind and the right attitude. When you are right-minded about what the Bible says about money, and recognize God's abundance is available to you, it changes the trajectory of your path to financial freedom.

What, then, is the healthy way to view wealth and material possessions? Why does the Bible caution against the love of money rather than money itself? Because the lure of money can be corruptive. Devastatingly so. As with all things that can take our affection away from Himself, God provides warnings, safeguards, and responsible guidelines for using money, and for protecting ourselves from its negative influence.

A Necessary Tool

Money is simply a tool. Just like any other tool, it is neither inherently good nor evil. Its use and impact depend on the heart condition, i.e. the motives, of those who possess it and wield its power. Money is necessary. Without it, life can be very difficult. For people unable to afford a decent place to live and purchase food, clothing, or medicine for their families, to say life is difficult is an understatement.

The same is true on a larger scale. How are projects funded, new ideas and concepts brought to life, organizations run, nations developed? It all takes money. It is virtually impossible to go through each day without making a decision that doesn't involve a financial consideration.

Money gives us choices. Among them are the choice of where to live, where to send our children to school, and which jobs to take. These are all potentially life-altering decisions. They affect our peace of mind in the moment, and the way our lives turn out in the long run. Even decisions of less importance are affected by whether we can afford to pay. Most people would choose differently if they had the money to vacation when and where they'd like, dress in the manner they prefer, and give to the causes that are important to them.

Money also provides access. This includes access to various experiences, circles, and ideas. One of the best ways to expand one's vision is by exposure. Seeing possibilities in spheres different from our own causes us to dream bigger and reach higher. Having access to greater opportunities is a way of opening the door to others and helping them to realize their own potential. Those of us who grew up in working-class families, or perhaps are first generation college graduates, experienced this on our college campuses. There, we were exposed to new ideas, learned of careers previously unknown, and formed relationships that broadened our horizons beyond a mere academic experience. We got access to resources we never knew existed, which in turn helped us take advantage of phenomenal opportunities. These experiences were transformational. It is why parents seek out the best schools for their children so they can be well-equipped and have access to the best opportunities in life.

The Lord desires our heart above all else. As long as the Lord has our hearts, as long as we have His heart for people and the things that are important to Him, we are actively combating the potentially corruptive influence of money. If our priorities are in order, we will love God and love people rather than money. Our actions will demonstrate this. This is the lesson of the story of the rich young ruler mentioned above. His priorities were out of order. He loved all his possessions more than he loved God, so he was heartbroken at the thought of giving everything away. Money was an idol in his life. Contrast this young man to the examples of the "righteous rich" that are found in Scripture. Both Abraham and Isaac are listed in Hebrews 11 among the heroes of faith. Solomon's kingdom was unsurpassed in greatness, and he flourished until his heart was turned away from God. These individuals, in addition to the ones mentioned in the New Testament, were committed to God, and fulfilled the calling on their lives. They also enjoyed the blessings of prosperity, while being generous and impacting the lives of those around them.

The conclusion to be drawn from all of this is that money is a necessary tool that gives us the power to shape our lives, and the world around us. For every story you've heard about the ills of being wealthy, there are a thousand more you haven't heard about the good that's done when honorable, noble-minded people use their wealth for the good of humanity.

> *Blessed are the right-minded,*
> *for they shall see the truth.*

In this chapter, we talked about the importance of having the right mindset to develop a healthy relationship with money and wealth creation. This includes having a right-minded view of God as the generous creator and owner of all things, a right-minded view of yourself as the beloved of God who is worthy to receive His financial blessings and capable of multiplying what He has given, and a right-minded view of money as a necessary tool for everyday living.

BE PRAYERFUL

Father, you are a God of abundance and unlimited resources. Help me eliminate negative thinking and renew my mind as it relates to financial freedom. Allow me to be right-minded about money by knowing there is nothing wrong with being a Christian who has access to Your abundance. Help me to see myself as worthy and capable of using the talents and gifts You have blessed me with to change my financial situation for the better. Amen.

BE DOERS

1. Be specific about something you need to unlearn and replace with the proper perspective. Is it about God, yourself, or money?

2. Think about ways that your upbringing has influenced your views on God. Does this line up with what He says about Himself in the Bible?

3. Find a few verses that speak about the attributes of God, specifically His love and His provision, and commit them to memory. Remind yourself of these truths every time you start to doubt.

Chapter 2

BE A GOOD STEWARD

Blessed are the good stewards,
for they shall be rewarded with more.

Brian, the Jamaican television executive we introduced in the last chapter, began his journey to establish a religious television channel with no resources and no experience in the field. All he had was an opportunity given by his friend. Instead of declining the offer or throwing up his hands in defeat, Brian collected and aired video tapes of sermons, concerts, and any other Christian content he could find. He reached out to people and asked to borrow whatever materials they had. Slowly, the programming for his young endeavor trickled in. The channel began to grow and caught the attention of more people, who offered more assistance. Eventually, the channel amassed a diverse lineup because he had so much new content. Because Brian did not despise his small beginnings, but instead worked faithfully with the few resources he possessed, he is now the operator of one of the largest Christian television networks in the Caribbean. The network is so successful that he has received multi-million-dollar offers from entities in the U.S. to buy it. Brian has been a good steward. He was faithful with the few resources he was given and now has many, many more.

Faithful stewardship is our next key to growing wealth biblically. What does it mean to be a steward? It simply means to be a manager of another's property. In this instance, it means that we are the managers or caretakers of God's wealth. This chapter will frequently refer to concepts introduced in chapter 1 because our status as stewards flows from God's status as owner. He allows us to use what really belongs to Him, with the expectation we will be faithful in managing what has been entrusted to our care. Faithful stewardship means managing someone else's belongings with the same or greater care than the owner would exercise themself. The apostle Paul wrote in 1 Corinthians 4:2 that "it is required in stewards that one be found faithful." In what ways can we be faithful managers of God's money?

RETURN TO GOD THAT WHICH BELONGS TO HIM

We believe the first way to *Be a Good Steward* is to practice tithing. Although this perspective is not universally shared in all Christian circles, we believe that tithing is foundational to managing God's money and that He still expects it of us. Tithing is both a sign of our obedience to God's commandment and a demonstration of our trust in His faithfulness to take care of our needs.

The tithe, which means *a tenth*, is the portion of earnings that is returned back to God. The tithe is first mentioned in Genesis 14 where Abram offers ten percent of his increase to Melchizedek, the priest of God Most High (see Genesis 14:18–20). The practice is mentioned throughout the Old and New Testaments (see Malachi 3:8–9, Matthew 23:23, and Hebrews 7:1–10). In Leviticus, for example, it says, "And all the tithe of the land, whether of the seed of the land or of the fruit of the tree, is the Lord's. It is holy to the Lord" (Leviticus 27: 30). Proverbs encourages God's people to "honor the Lord with your possessions, and with the firstfruits of all your increase" (Proverbs 3:9). Since these verses were written to a largely agrarian society, "firstfruits" or "first fruits" referenced setting aside the first crops and livestock that were produced for God. Today, because increase comes in the form of wages, tithers contribute ten percent of their income to their local church. Some refer to it as "paying God first." The point is that before spending our earnings on anything else, the first 10 percent is immediately reserved and returned to God through our local church.

The frequent and rich conversations (no pun intended) we had around tithing with our wealthy interviewees took us completely by surprise. Because we did not ask specific questions about tithing, not all the interviewees shared whether they adhered to this practice. However, the ones that did share spoke passionately about the subject without prompting and resoundingly affirmed committing to the principle of tithing as one reason for their financial success.

Gina, a multi-millionaire from Buffalo, New York, drew us in with her high-energy, candid, and detailed recounting of her life. Her remarkable story about how she amassed wealth through shrewd, largely self-taught investing was captivating and inspiring. But according to her, the key that transformed her life was a long-standing commitment to tithing. Gina began tithing on a dare. Her former pastor levied the challenge every year at the church's annual January revival. According to her, every year he preached a sermon on tithing and dared members of the congregation to begin the year tithing and see what God would do. After hearing about this dare for quite a few years, Gina decided to take the challenge. This was a life-changing decision that she has never regretted.

The idea of framing tithing as a dare did not originate with Gina's pastor. The Prophet Malachi wrote that God Himself dared the children of Israel to tithe. He literally says, "Try Me now in this" (Malachi 3:10) and promises an outpouring of blessing in return. Gina, now a tither for several decades, excitedly shared that because she has been faithful in this area, God has met and surpassed her every need.

Gina's story resonated with and encouraged us to remain committed to tithing. As a young believer, Fania fully embraced tithing and practiced it for most of her earning years. However, as seasons of financial challenge arose and bills started piling up, she began to have conversations with herself about how important tithing really was. These conversations went something like this, "The mortgage and power companies won't understand if they're not paid this month, but God will understand." Or sometimes, "Forgoing tithing in the lean times is okay if it's made up when things get better." At other times, she would ease her conscience by rationalizing that since she was helping to support others who were in need, it was okay to not give to the church that week.

Maybe you can relate. In the face of present difficulties or temptations, disobedience to God can seem to have distant consequences. This is far from the truth. There are very real consequences of disobedience. In Fania's experience, the years in which she faithfully tithed were marked by financial blessings and provision. As the One who truly owns everything, God is both willing and able to give us not just what we need, but also what we want. During the times when she

While God is the ultimate decision-maker in how resources are distributed, He also allows us to participate in our own success by how well we steward what He has entrusted to us.

was not faithful in her giving, scarcity continued and bills and other "devourers" the book of Malachi speaks about seemed to materialize from everywhere (see Malachi 3:11). God still blessed her throughout the lean times because He is just that good, but she did not experience the peace nor the ease that she did when she tithed faithfully. Cassandra agreed. She and her husband committed to tithing early in their marriage based on both the examples of their parents and their desire to be obedient to the Lord. "For us it's a nonnegotiable part of how we manage our finances." Cassandra shared, "We are committed to tithing as a core value of our faith, but we've also experienced the amazing provision of God as we have acted on our obedience." In applying the lessons learned and reinforced during the process of writing this book, our commitment to faithful tithing has been strengthened and affirmed. What about you? Are you willing to accept the challenge and make tithing a part of your lifestyle?

GROW WHAT YOU HAVE BEEN GIVEN

There's Enough for Everyone

In the first chapter, we discussed one of two important principles from the parable of the talents, namely that as creator and owner of everything, God decides how gifts and resources are distributed. The second principle from the parable of the talents is that the actions and choices of the servants themselves (that's us!) can impact whether the number of resources they receive will increase. There is so much power in this story for us because it means that while God is the ultimate decision-maker in how resources are distributed, He also allows us to participate in our own success by how well we steward what He has entrusted to us. Consider the master's response to the servant who buried his talent and returned it without any increase. "You wicked and lazy servant!" he said (Matthew 25:26). This indictment was reserved for the servant who failed to handle the talent the way the master would have himself. Jesus's encouragement to multiply our financial resources, as opposed to allowing them to languish, teaches us that God expects us to grow what we have been given.

One of the impediments to multiplying our blessings may be our own mindset. Many of us approach our finances with the thought that there's a limited number of blessings to go around, and if some of us get so many, then others have to go without. The truth is that many people will go without, but not because there isn't enough for everyone. The root of this belief is that many believers have a hard time with the concept of abundance. It evokes images of excessive or wasteful living. This self-limiting thinking sometimes leads to lack and scarcity, while others enjoy abundance. In order to *Be a Good Steward*, we must approach opportunities to grow our financial assets with a mindset of abundance.

Abundance is part of the nature of God. We challenge you to think about the vastness and diversity of creation. Thinking of all that God has created is impossible because at any given moment we only see a small portion of what exists. New galaxies are still being discovered! There are many verses that talk about God's treasury and abundance. Consider David's praise for God in Psalm 65:11, where he acknowledges the resources of God and that He "crown[s] the year with [His] goodness, and [His] paths drip with abundance." In 2 Corinthians 9:8 it says that God is able to bless you abundantly so that in all things, at all times, you will have what you need. These verses tell us that God is not limited in His resources. He will never run out of resources since He Himself is limitless. What does this have to do with our money? If we think of money as another resource that God provides, we will not be held captive by thoughts of scarcity. There isn't a finite number of blessings to go around. God is generous.

Invest... It's Not Just for Rich White Men

Growing up in New York City, buildings bearing the names of industrial age titans like Rockefeller, Carnegie, Morgan, and Vanderbilt were the backdrop for many field trips, workshops, and science and college fairs. We grew up hearing these names and referring to their landmarks long before we understood their lasting impact on the city. But the success of these men, like the stock market and investing they had mastered, seemed far out of reach for us. Wealth achieved by investing seemed to be the exclusive domain of White men. Our proximity to Wall Street and the buildings, where multi-billion-dollar deals were being made, was not enough to impress upon us that wealth creation through investing was possible.

Unfortunately, our initial views of investing persist within the Black community. National statistics still show that Black people are significantly underrepresented as investors compared to their White counterparts and, according to the Ariel-Schwab Black Investor Survey, Black Americans are more likely to express distrust of banks and investing institutions.[1]

Gina's story stands as a sharp contrast against this disparity. Gina, as we noted earlier in the chapter, first inspired us with her commitment to the tithe. However, she also has a remarkable story of successfully amassing millions of dollars through careful saving and investing in the stock market. As a Black woman, Gina for years dealt with being significantly underpaid compared to her White co-workers. Ironically, much of this injustice came to light after her White colleagues and employer faced legal charges for an illegal overtime payment scheme that she, thankfully, was also excluded from. Gina decided to learn about investing as a means of improving her financial situation for retirement. Although she worked full-time as an anesthesiologist, she felt the years of discriminatory underpayment left her unprepared for retirement. She decided to self-educate on investing by building her own personal library of finance books and studying materials from magazines and leading experts in the investment field. She also prioritized saving over spending. Gina acknowledged that if given the choice between saving and spending, she would choose saving, admitting that she's called "painfully frugal" by her sister.

When Gina made the decision to educate herself about investing in order to pursue an intentional strategy of becoming rich, she wasn't overly confident in her ability to succeed, and as might be expected, she made many early mistakes. "I subscribed to some newsletters. One of those newsletters gave a model portfolio that encouraged investors to put money in gold. And I lost half of my money. Well, first of all the money doubled, and then I lost half. And then I wasn't smart enough to get out before I lost most of that," Gina shared candidly. Undeterred, Gina persisted in learning from and exposing herself to other investors. She explained, "I finally got around to Vanguard with the index funds. And I also joined the American Association of Individual Investors (AAII) and got better investing magazines." Her voracious reading and investment in her own personal understanding eventually led to her making better investment decisions. Gina's commitment to being an informed steward paid off, and she now has a well-endowed retirement fund.

Whether it's investing in the stock market or real estate, there is room for everyone at the table. God's blessings are not limited to any race, gender, or nationality. Wise investing is a strategy open to anyone willing to put in the time necessary to learn to grow their assets and yield increase. Although Gina chose to manage her own funds, there are also many reputable investment advisors and institutions that can be trusted to assist in managing your investment portfolio.

Avoid Debt

The Bible is clear on the pitfalls of debt. Proverbs 22:7 states, "The rich rules over the poor, and the borrower is servant to the lender." Equating borrowing money to slavery or imprisonment seems harsh, but in reality, the quickest and surest way to derail our goals of wealth attainment is to become mired in debt. When we are in debt, we are not free. Reverend DeForest B. Soaries, Jr., founder of the Dfree Movement, notes that consumer debt, which he refers to as plastic shackles, has taken a heavy toll on millions of Americans, and especially the Black community. Soaries notes that, "Consumer debt enslaves millions of people in our country with debilitating chains that only seem to grow tighter each month as bills increase and income decreases. We've shackled ourselves with fear, stress, and shame by spending far more than we're taking in or saving."[2] Dr. Soaries's groundbreaking work focuses on using a Scripture-based, comprehensive strategy of education, planning, and accountability to guide individuals and families toward financial freedom. Freedom from debt is possible, but it takes discipline and countercultural living to avoid the lure and persistent schemes of credit card companies and big business and to reject the "buy now and pay later" mentality that targets even the youngest among us.

Anna, the co-owner of an engineering firm, credits her parents with instilling the discipline of living within her means from a young age. In her interview, she recounted the story of her sister applying for a credit card while in college and the card being mailed to their home. Her father was not happy and gave her sister a "tongue lashing," telling her, "We don't do credit cards." Instead, Anna and her sister were made authorized users on their father's American Express charge card, which required them to pay the balance in full every month. Her current membership dates back to that day.

Although Anna's parents were not well-educated, she values their practical common sense as demonstrated in the lessons they taught, as well as how they lived their own lives. Anna's parents were working-class, her mother a secretary and her father a sales representative, but they instilled in her the invaluable lesson that even without a large salary, a person can live comfortably, as long as he or she lives within their means. Living paycheck to paycheck was anathema to her family's beliefs. "That just taught me right then and there, I don't need a new car when I graduate from college. I don't need to buy new clothes all the time in the latest styles," Anna shared.

Some of us had to learn the pitfalls of consumer debt the hard way. Anna's parents helped her and her sister avoid falling into a trap that many of us first generation college students fell into during our earliest days on college campuses. Like many of our friends, Cassandra can still remember applying for her first credit card, not because she needed anything, but because she was offered a free t-shirt in the student union. Later credit card acquisitions were made to get something as simple as a discount of a few percentage points on a minor purchase. Credit card companies and predatory vendors intentionally target young, inexperienced, and financially illiterate youth before they even get started in professional careers. Their simple strategies remain incredibly effective. These ploys are really just variations of the same basic promise: buy now, pay later. Sadly, we are being sold a lie. The truth is that debt enslaves us. True financial freedom comes through avoiding debt and developing discipline.

Practice Integrity in Financial Affairs

Being a good steward of the resources we've been given also means we should be ethical in the ways we use money. Financial ethics may not be included in the many books about attaining wealth. However, the Bible is clear about its importance in both personal and business relationships. Being ethical in business practices was a common instruction God gave to the children of Israel, and He still expects it of His followers. In Scripture, there are prohibitions against charging excessive interest, instructions concerning the fair treatment of workers, and admonishments about caring for the poor. Solomon wrote, "Wealth gained by dishonesty will be diminished, but he who gathers by labor will increase" (Proverbs 13:11). The king's words issue a stark warning, which should inform the methods we use to make money, and the way we treat others with whom we engage in business transactions. The consequence of dishonesty is not only financial loss but also the Lord's displeasure with us, arousing His vengeance on behalf of those who have been treated unfairly.

Our businesses, and even our daily affairs, must be carried out in alignment with the values we profess. It's easy to see how blatant, high-profile cases of fraud are wrong, but we must guard against this behavior in our everyday lives. All of us must resist the lure of sin to make a quick buck. Malcolm is the pastor of one of the fastest growing churches in the United States, a successful real estate entrepreneur, and well-regarded civil rights leader. He is also a dear friend of

Cassandra's family, who over the years has consistently exemplified integrity in his faith and personal walk. We specifically sought him out because of his success in multiple arenas, and his deep commitment to preaching and teaching the gospel. Pastor Malcolm offered valuable insight on maintaining integrity in business. Here is what he shared: "I've learned the discipline of searching my heart to make sure the right things are driving me... I'm operating in kingdom principles. So, the principles are the good guardrails." Pastor Malcolm stated, "What I've really come to appreciate is that business, no matter what type, is, at the end of the day, about people. And I've learned to do business with people whom I respect. I prefer for them to be believers, but if they can't be believers, they at least have to be people I think have integrity."

Pastor Malcolm's words offer guidance in a couple of ways. First, it highlights our responsibility to monitor our own actions to make sure they are aboveboard. Second, and perhaps surprising for some, is our responsibility to make sure that those with whom we engage in business are also acting ethically. Why is this important? Because unscrupulous business practices affect our witness and ultimately our outcome. If we engage with others who are being dishonest, we are essentially validating that behavior. We cannot then claim to have clean hands. Also, remember the scriptural admonition that wealth gained by dishonesty will be diminished. By joining ourselves together in a dishonest financial venture, we are setting ourselves up for failure.

Being good stewards of the money God has entrusted to us involves operating with integrity in our financial dealings. This extends beyond our own behavior. It includes avoiding doing business with those who are themselves dishonest. If we are in business with corrupt people, we will be seen as corrupt ourselves.

"I live debt free. I believe in investing in stocks and property. Make your money work . Don't just put it in the bank. When you do this, you don't have to work as hard. It frees up time to do God's work." The speaker of these words was Brian, the Caribbean television executive that we began the chapter with. Brian's philosophy of managing his money aligns well with the practice and the ultimate reward of being a good steward.

Blessed are the good stewards,
for they shall be rewarded with more.

God created all things and is the owner of all things. He allows us to be stewards, or managers, over his creation, which includes wealth. An important part of being good stewards is tithing, as a sign of our obedience to and trust in God. We are responsible for, and capable of, increasing what we've been given with care and integrity.

BE PRAYERFUL

Father, I want to be a good steward of all the things You've given me. I recognize that all I have is Yours, but You've entrusted it to my care. Please help me to be a faithful caretaker of Your resources by tithing, being ethical in my financial dealings, and growing what You've given me. Amen.

BE DOERS

1. Read and accept the challenge of Malachi 3:10. Find ways to increase what God has already given you.

2. Educate yourself on investing and other opportunities to grow your financial assets.

3. Avoid debt and practice discipline in using credit.

4. Operate with honesty and integrity in your financial dealings.

BE SPIRIT-LED

Blessed are the Spirit-led,
for they shall walk in God's will.

Very soon after entering law school, Fania realized she didn't want to practice law. However, after investing the time and money in getting there, and because she didn't have a clear idea of what she did want to do, she decided to complete the program, instead of what she considered would be quitting. After graduating, she had no clearer idea of her direction, and now with the burden of student loans, she sought a position at a law firm. A few years in she was well compensated, well regarded, and utterly miserable. So, she decided to quit her job and pursue…. well, she didn't know exactly what. She had a few interests, and the advice of many that "you can do anything with a law degree." Furthermore, she believed she had God's blessing in quitting, because surely it wasn't His will for her to be unhappy and unfulfilled. Within a year, she was depleting her savings, getting into debt, and still had no clearer path forward. The initial freedom and joy she experienced upon leaving a stressful job were replaced by mounting anxiety caused by her uncertain future. How had she gotten into this predicament? What had she missed? And perhaps more importantly, how could she get herself out of this increasingly dire situation? Let's pause here for a bit and turn our attention back to you and your life.

How do you make decisions? How do you figure out what to do when faced with questions in your career, business, or life in general? How do you know if you are living in the will of God? We know these are weighty questions. They are the same ones we've both wrestled with at different points throughout our lives. The answers to these questions were central to Fania's ability to course correct at that low point in her career. Reminiscing on these early years, Fania recounted, "In my earnest desire to 'do what I was created to do' and 'follow after God's plan,' I missed the practical, commonsense, written Word that was right in front of me." She continued, "As I sought the Lord about how to get myself out of the mess I had created, I sensed He was directing me to the question He had asked Moses all those centuries ago. I was to use what was in my hand." Fania was referring to the scene in Exodus where the Lord redirected Moses's anxious questions about how he would be received by the Egyptians by asking him "What is that in your hand?" (Exodus 4:2). After Moses replied that he held a rod, the Lord showed him he was already equipped to accomplish his assignment. In Fania's case, the Lord's reassurance directed her to use her legal training to rebuild her career.

Our third *Be Attitude, Be Spirit-Led*, is key to both knowing and walking in God's will for our lives. Being Spirit-led marks our identity as followers of Christ and our continuous, active commitment to allow God to guide our decision-making and actions. Being Spirit-led acknowledges that despite our best efforts to make sound decisions, we are incapable of choosing the best path using our own wisdom alone. Unlike our all-knowing, all-seeing heavenly Father, we are limited in our ability to take in, much less make sense of, our current reality. This is because personal biases, emotions, miscalculations, and other factors that mark us as humans cloud our ability to accurately read a situation and make completely informed decisions. We can't tell the future or predict with one hundred percent certainty the best path to guarantee our preferred outcome. In contrast, our faith is built on the assurance that God has our best interest in mind, and if we place our trust in Him, He will both guide our steps and work our circumstances together for our good. Solomon said, "Trust in the Lord with all your heart, and lean not to your own understanding; in all your ways acknowledge Him, and He shall direct your paths" (Proverbs 3:5–6).

A SPIRIT-LED LIFESTYLE

At its core, being Spirit led is a lifestyle born out of an abiding personal relationship with Christ. According to Romans 8:14, submitting to the leading of the Spirit distinguishes us from the world and identifies us as children of God. As His children, we are committing to a lifestyle where the Lord's will is sought and prioritized. This commitment is countercultural. Unlike aspects of the other *Be Attitudes* we discuss, you won't find *Be Spirit-Led* in popular financial planning books or success manuals. Nevertheless, for the believer, this way of living must be paramount. Don't skip this chapter or allow your eyes to glaze over as you read. Read on slowly and carefully while inviting the Holy Spirit to lead and guide you in His will. After all, that's the point!

You may be familiar with the story of young Samuel, who thought a voice calling his name as he lay in bed in the middle of the night was his mentor, Eli's. Each time Samuel heard his name being called, he ran to Eli and said, "Here I am, for you called me" (1 Samuel 3:5). Even though Samuel had grown up in the temple and had "ministered to the Lord before Eli" (v. 1) almost his entire life, he still didn't recognize God's voice. This may not seem noteworthy to you. He was, after all, still a boy. However, as we continue to read, we learn "the word of the Lord was rare in those days; there was no widespread revelation" (v. 1). Further still, we are told, "Now Samuel did not yet know the Lord, nor was the word of the Lord yet revealed to Him" (v. 7).

We have an advantage today Samuel could not have imagined. Samuel lived at a time before Jesus's arrival on earth provided the perfect example of a Spirit-led life. He also lived before God sent us the Holy Spirit to permanently dwell within us to empower and guide us toward His will. Finally, Samuel lived without the full written Word of God through which today we gain a great understanding of the character and heart of God. We have full access to it all. By following the example of Christ, obeying the Word of God in Scripture, and yielding to the Holy Spirit, we can cultivate a Spirit-led lifestyle.

The Importance of Bible Study

Twenty-first-century living can be noisy, hectic, and fast-paced. Carving out time for regular and consistent Bible study is essential for cutting through the noise, so we can understand how the Spirit is leading. In his book, *The Mystery of God's Will*, Charles Swindoll states, "The better you get to know the Word of God, the less confusing is the will of God. Those who struggle least with the will of God are the ones who know the Word of God best."[3] The books, songs, and stories encapsulated in the Bible are designed to reveal God's character to us. Through His written Word we can learn how He expects us to live, think, interact with Him, and treat others. The Bible also shares God's unwavering love for all of humanity and tells how He made provision so we can all have a sincere, intimate relationship with Him. Knowing the Bible for ourselves will keep us firmly grounded in the true knowledge of God. Moreover, through Bible study, we hone our ability to identify the paths that bring us closer to God and those we should avoid.

The Importance of Prayer

Prayer is also important in understanding the will of God. Spending time in prayer hones our capacity to hear the voice of the Lord and follow His Spirit. Recently, our church completed a study on prayer using Pete Greig's beautifully written book, *How to Pray: A Simple Guide for Normal People*. In it, Greig likens prayer to a "complex, living landscape" that we journey through with the Lord.[4] He writes: "There's no one superior way to pray... But, as you set out on the many paths of prayer, the Lord is going to join you on the journey... He's going to walk in silence with you, and talk with you, too. The conversation will ebb and flow. He will tell you things you never knew and ask you things you've never been told."[5] Pete uses the example of the Lord's Prayer to introduce nine different types of prayers that help structure and improve our prayer lives. However, the fundamental takeaway from this book and, more importantly, the Scriptures, is that God invites us to join Him in prayer. He delights in this communion no matter how inelegant, unprepared, or unworthy we feel in those moments. As Pete states repeatedly in his book, we just need to "keep it simple, keep it real, and keep it up!"[6]

Jenna, an entrepreneur and owner of a technology and marketing company, gave us a glimpse into her morning routine based on her commitment to prayer. For decades, she has awakened at 3:00 a.m., for an hour of prayer and thanksgiving. She considers this time critical to her living into the woman she desires to be. It's also an opportunity for her to intercede for business clients and ask for God's guidance on how to run her company. She shared: "But honestly, it might as well be like a business meeting for me. I lift up to the Lord, 'Okay, Father. I got this situation,' or 'You know, Lord, how are we gonna get this done?'" Jenna told us that because she expects the Lord to answer her prayers, she also makes time to listen for His reply. She reported, "And then in my mind it is wide open. I see no reason why the same God that can inform Steve Jobs can't inform me directly. I don't need to go through anybody. So, anything that I'm doing, I can go directly to the Lord, and I have the time, I have His ear."

Jenna eloquently explained that her time of prayer is vital to strengthening her relationship with the Lord. We have found the same to be true when we have nurtured our own prayer lives. Consistently making time to pray, study, and commune with the Lord draws us closer to Him so we can be attuned to His will. This time also makes room for God to transform our character and disposition, so we are more inclined to be led by His Spirit.

A SPIRIT-LED HEART

Knowing God's heart should lead us to another important question: does God have *my* heart? Although this question seems straightforward, it is not always easy to answer. When it comes to matters of the heart, sometimes we see what we want to see and believe what we want to believe, usually with the perception that we are better than we actually are. Self-enhancement bias is a common blind spot in all adults. As a result of this skewed perspective, we believe we are more righteous than we are, and seemingly virtuous actions may be inspired by less than honorable motives. One way to get a truly accurate picture of our heart condition is to allow the Spirit Himself to search us and reveal what we tend to obscure with the performance of good deeds, saying the right things, and going through the motions of being a "good Christian." With His help, we can truly know what has priority in our lives, what has our attention, and what we value.

You are not alone in needing to do this heart check. When we first began writing this book, we made it a point of prayer that God would keep before us "the main thing," which for us is our relationship with Him, and fulfilling the call He has on our lives. For both of us, becoming wealthy is *a* goal, but it is not *the* goal. This distinction is not insignificant. It is central to our premise. Being wealthy doesn't guarantee one will be happy, peaceful, or free from problems. Just think about the many stories you've heard about wealthy individuals who deal with and sometimes succumb to addictions, illnesses, and a variety of other struggles. We believe true satisfaction, joy, and peace are found in Christ. That is why it is important for us to keep the first things first.

Allowing the Spirit to lead in this continuous heart inventory is critical, as we work to build our wealth profile. If you are unsure of where your heart lies, ask for the Spirit's guidance. Even for those who are sure, checking in with God is a good practice to develop. Know, however, that once we invite the Lord to search our hearts, it may lead to some surprising and uncomfortable discoveries. He may just go into areas we didn't intend. He is thorough and will enter areas of

God will not lead or direct us to manage our finances in ways that are inconsistent with his precepts and character.

our heart we have firmly bolted shut and affixed with "do not tres-pass" signs. He will show us the truth. His searching will reveal feel-ings, desires, and motives that may be invisible to others, or even to ourselves. As uncomfortable as this may seem, don't let it stop you from allowing Him in. His touch is gentle and loving, rather than rough and bruising. His goal is to reveal the truth and to restore.

Although the Spirit leads the search, we can and should be active participants in evaluating the condition of our heart. With all we have going on in our lives, where does Christ fit in? What or who receives our attention, money, creativity, and energy? This should not be a philosophical exercise. Check the record. If you haven't already experienced discomfort in this exercise, this is where things can get really uncomfortable. What is revealed by our checkbooks, bank state-ments, calendars, journals, social media feed, reading logs, and playl-ists? Seeing the undeniable record of our habits and affections can be hard to take in, especially if it reveals we are living in a way that is not consistent with the values and priorities we profess. But remember, the Spirit's goal is never to leave us exposed and ashamed. His goal is to lovingly correct and restore us to the right path, where our rela-tionship with Christ is our priority, and we are aligned with His will.

SPIRIT-LED DECISION-MAKING

The "how-to" of Christian decision-making is typically presented as a process of seeking God's will through prayer, gathering information, assessing options based on biblical principles, and seeking the wisdom of trusted advisors. As we explained earlier, Spirit-led decision-mak-ing is an outgrowth of a Spirit-led lifestyle, fueled by time regularly spent in the presence of God. Lifestyle decisions about money and finances are ever present in this framework. The reality is that most of our daily decisions involve finances, and money matters are inextricably woven into the very fabric of our lives. When it comes to making decisions, whether explicitly tied to money or not, we should know that God has an opinion and something to say. As His children, we have full access to His Spirit to guide our decision-making.

Implicit in the step of seeking God's will through prayer is the assumption that we care about His will. That is, what He desires for us. In other words, we want to know His heart on the matter. Knowing the heart of God is the first step in making sure we are being led by His Spirit. We are not suggesting this is always an easy process. Decisions about money are unique to the individual and will be based on what you hear from God. Even mature believers can sometimes question whether the prompting they feel is the Spirit leading them along a certain path, the advice of another trusted counselor, or their own desire to go that way. Or what if, after praying, we still don't have a specific answer to the question we've asked? What if there are several doors open to us and there's no flashing green light above the one God wants us to walk through? Discernment on this level is grounded in the consistent nature of God, but it's also personal and individualized. We know from our own lives and those of the men and women we interviewed that God speaks to us individually and leads us in ways that are specific to our situation. However, we also know there are aspects of His will that are universal. This is why spending time with God in Bible study and learning to discern His voice is so critical.

Knowing the will of God and learning to distinguish the voice of His Spirit from the many loud voices that seek to influence us can be a daunting prospect. Yet it is doable. We were given some rich, practical, real-life examples of these truths when we sat down to speak with Michelle Singletary, a financial expert, well respected in faith and secular communities alike. Michelle is a best-selling author, award-winning columnist for the *Washington Post*, and head of the financial ministry at the First Baptist Church of Glenarden, an expansive ministry in Prince George's County, Maryland, with over twenty thousand members. Her column, *The Color of Money*, is carried by newspapers across the United States, and her books on money have guided millions of people from all walks of life. Saving, investing, and making wise financial decisions are prominent themes in her personal, professional, and spiritual life. In other words, she knows what she is talking about.

As Michelle eloquently highlighted for us, God will not lead or direct us to manage our finances in ways that are inconsistent with his precepts and character. She offered several scenarios to illustrate this point, but one particular incident from her own life really helped to make it clear. She was approached by a network to be featured in a TV show. The deal included a move from the Washington, DC, area to Los Angeles for filming. On the surface it appeared to be a great deal - it was lucrative, high profile, and could have potentially allowed Michelle to reach many more people and increase her platform and her presence. Ultimately, Michelle turned down the deal because she was attuned to the Spirit and recognized that the opportunity was not the right path for her, her family, and her marriage. Here's what she had to say on the topic: "You have to know how to hear the voice of God and when He's saying no, and when He's saying yes, and that's so individual." Michelle told us, "The key is if the rest of your life is being destroyed by your pursuit of something, then I think that's God saying no. Because along the way—if you're destroying your marriage, if you have a horrible relationship with your children—those are signs that that's not God talking because He wouldn't do that. He wouldn't destroy your family. He wouldn't destroy your marriage. He's a believer in marriage. He's a believer in family. And if those things are being damaged, then that is not the path."

Michelle had some direct advice for entrepreneurs that we found especially impactful. "When I talk to entrepreneurs and people who want to be entrepreneurs and see them running themselves ragged and making their families broke trying to pursue a business proposition that just isn't happening, I think God is saying, 'Nope, that's not for you.'" Michelle shared, "I spoke to this attorney who wanted to have her own practice, but she wasn't making any money, and she was going broke using credit cards. And I'm like, 'You know, you need to get a job! I don't care what you want to do.' *He is clear.* If this is something He wants you to do, He will provide. He will make the resources happen."

We were intrigued by Michelle's interview, especially her assertion that God is clear. Her statement reinforced the point we made earlier in this chapter that our God is knowable. He derives no pleasure watching us from afar, as we fumble around trying to understand His will. Hearing God's voice, and what He's saying to us as individuals, begins with a knowledge of who God is and what He values. This is based on principles He's already set out in His Word, such as putting Him first, family order, stewardship, and many other topics we will delve into in later chapters. The more familiar we are with those principles, the better positioned we are to stay or get aligned with His will. He speaks and consistently leads us to stay, and remain, in His will.

Stella, a successful businesswoman, defying the odds in the male-dominated construction industry, provided us with yet another compelling portrait of someone intent on being Spirit-led. Stella's success has been featured in major publications such as *Essence, Ebony*, and *Black Enterprise*. But in 1996 she was just a young adult, recently graduated from college and trying to figure out what to do with her life. She described that moment as being at a crossroads, facing one of the most challenging decisions of her life. The choices were whether to enroll in graduate school to become a big-time lawyer or to start her own business in the construction industry, in the footsteps of her father. Here is how she ultimately decided: "I remember how I made the decision. I remember it was through prayer and through a lot of reflection. But how I really made the final decision was when I saw that crossroad before me. It was just like God showed me, 'You can do the JD-MBA, and you will be fine. You will be successful. You will be fine. There's nothing bad that can happen to you if you take this road. But if you take the road I'm showing you, I'm going to take you to places you've never dreamed.'"

Perhaps most people who were evaluating Stella's options would have thought that enrolling in graduate school was the right decision for her at that time. After all, a typical path for many young adults is enrollment in graduate school after college. Many others pursue full-time employment working in someone else's business. A young Black woman starting a construction company right out of college propelled Stella to unicorn status! With God all things are possible. Stella's story exemplifies that being Spirit-led hinges on our capacity to trust that God has our best interests at heart, even when we don't understand what He is doing, and when the odds are stacked against us. As we spend more time with Him, we also learn to trust our own ability to discern His voice, especially when it goes against conventional wisdom.

What If We Miss It?

What happens if we believe we've heard from God, act upon what we've heard, and don't get the results we thought we would? Is it possible to have a close relationship with God—to know His Word and pray consistently—and still make the wrong decision? The answer is yes. This very thing has caused many believers to doubt their ability to hear from God or doubt that He actually speaks to them. It may even cause them to doubt other decisions they've made in the past, and induce a state of paralysis in future decision-making. How do we overcome this?

The first step is to reaffirm our belief in God's goodness and His love for us. This should always be our true north. The second step is to seek Him, acknowledge our feelings of disappointment, and ask Him to show us where we went wrong. Next, we ask for His guidance in getting back on the right path, be receptive to what He is saying to us, and obey.

There's great comfort in knowing God is a restorer. Remember, His desire is not to condemn us but to correct us and lead us back to the right path. Making financial missteps doesn't have to be the end of our journey to wealth building.

> *Blessed are the Spirit-led,*
> *for they shall walk in God's will.*

Being Spirit-led should be a lifestyle. The lifestyle is established by studying God's Word and spending time with Him in prayer. It is reinforced by asking His Spirit to do periodic heart checks to ensure we remain in alignment with Him. By doing these things we learn to recognize God's voice and are able to follow His guidance.

BE PRAYERFUL

God, you are the One who truly knows my heart. My desire is that I will be led by the Spirit. Help me prioritize my time, attention, and values, with You at the top of the list. I want to honor You in everything I do, including in how I manage what you have blessed me with. Amen.

BE DOERS

1. Set aside a dedicated time for regular personal Bible study and prayer.

2. Continuously invite the Spirit to search your heart to make sure your values and actions are aligned with God's will.

3. Seek God regularly before making decisions, in order to get in the habit of being led by the Spirit.

Chapter 4

BE BOLD

Blessed are the bold, for they
shall realize success beyond their dreams.

B e bold" was not an instruction regularly given to little girls when we were growing up. Be respectful, of course. Be nice, always. Be quiet, you better believe it. Be bold, never. To be called bold as a child in a Caribbean household, especially a female child, was akin to being called rude, disrespectful, or defiant. Bold was used to describe the child who talked back to her parents and other adults. It resulted in strict discipline and constant lectures about the sad end of children who acted this way.

The negative associations with this word *bold* were formed early in our minds and followed us into adulthood. They have affected our relationships with people and, yes, also with money. On-the-job raises were asked for reluctantly, if at all, salary negotiations filled us with dread, and business ideas were not pursued because they were deemed too risky.

As our interviews progressed, we began to see boldness in a different light. This newly emergent perspective helped us to identify, and to give a new appreciation to, the examples of boldness being lived out in our own families, and in many who were similarly situated. For example, Cassandra began to see the inspirational story of her own mother, who in her early twenties immigrated from the tiny Caribbean island of Grenada to the United States, in a new light. Cassandra recounted, "I hold my mother in high esteem and have always valued her sacrifice, but I never fully appreciated the courage and, yes, the boldness it took for her to initiate a change that would impact her entire family. I saw resilience, hard work, faithfulness, and so much more, but I didn't see boldness." She continued, "My mother is one of the humblest people I know, she would never credit herself in any way for the success our family has achieved because of her, let alone classify her deeds as bold. If she were asked, I am sure she would say, in her typical fashion, 'to God be the glory for giving me the strength.' I know better than to argue with her and there is no need. God *did* strengthen her, *and* she was bold. Both statements are true." At just twenty-one years old, against crushing odds, Cassandra's mother left her family and friends for a place unknown, to make a life for herself and her family. It wasn't easy, but through the grace of God she persisted and succeeded. Cassandra admitted, "It's hard to admit I didn't initially draw inspiration for boldness from her example."

Cassandra notes that her mother's boldness, although remarkable, is not unique. Many immigrants have similar stories. We highlight those of Caribbean women here because those are our stories—experiences shared by our mothers and countless other women. Although they weren't championing causes or building corporations, the boldness inherent in the radical actions of young, often unmarried women to take charge of their future is something we can recognize and honor.

Boldness is making a choice to act, to move toward opportunities, to overcome challenges, and to fulfill our dreams, even if it means doing so with knocking knees and sweaty palms!

Their acts of boldness, combined with God's faithfulness in providing and blessing, inspire us as we make our own financial moves from economic survival to financial freedom and thriving.

So, what do we really mean by *Be Bold*? The dictionary defines the word *bold* as "fearless before danger; intrepid," with secondary definitions such as "showing or requiring a fearless, daring spirit" and "assured, confident."[7] Words like *confident* and *intrepid* may imply, for some, that boldness is achieved without fear, failure, or danger. In fact, nothing could be further from the truth. Boldness is a recognition that feelings, especially how we view ourselves, no matter how strongly held, can be fickle, misleading, and sometimes dead wrong. Boldness can be increased. Boldness is making a choice to act, to move toward opportunities, to overcome challenges, and to fulfill our dreams, even if it means doing so with knocking knees and sweaty palms!

Be Bold is integral for building wealth and achieving success. This *Be Attitude* works especially well in concert with *Be Right-Minded* and *Be Spirit-Led*. It invites us all to apply the same type of resolve and confidence we have used in other successful areas of our lives to take charge of our finances and build wealth. This is where we get to work as an outgrowth of a right mindset and a faith that the Spirit is indeed leading and guiding. With this *Be Attitude*, we are affirming that *since*—rather than *if*—we are being led by the Spirit, we must choose to act and to shine. Breaking out of limiting financial practices to achieve wealth beyond what we can see or imagine will require us to be bold.

Moreover, *Be Bold* is reminiscent of the command seen repeatedly in Scripture that encourages Spirit-led persons to act or fulfill their assignment, especially in circumstances that are challenging or scary. From encouraging warriors, like Joshua, into battle, and leaders, like Moses, for the immense task of shepherding God's people, to strengthening the resolve of young preachers like Timothy to proclaim the gospel, the Bible details how the call for courage or boldness has encouraged different people to fulfill extraordinary service, or to take the first simple step towards a life of greatness. Boldness, however, is not reserved for the pages of the Bible, nor is it reserved for spiritual or military conquests. It can be applied to our everyday, ordinary lives.

BOLDNESS IS AN OUTGROWTH
OF BEING SPIRIT-LED

We were told, "I'm going to go where the opportunities are. That's what you do. You need to be a risk-taker. They need to be, I'd say, sort of reasonable risks. But you can't be afraid. You've got to step out and go places that you've not been to or that your relatives haven't been. If the opportunity looks right, if the Spirit is saying to you, 'This is a place and a direction you probably want to go,' you've got to go do it. You need to go do it." Reuben, the speaker of these words, was describing to us how he made decisions and principles that led to his successful career.

Reuben left his deeply segregated hometown of Jackson, Tennessee, with his mother and two siblings, for a new life in Gary, Indiana. It was the 1960's and, like many African American families of the time, the move was prompted by the search for economic opportunity. The tipping point came when Reuben's mother was denied a $5-a-week raise for her work as a grocery store cashier. This disappointment led her to finally accept the invitation of her brother, Reuben's uncle, to move to Gary to get a higher paying job at the steel mill. Two years after arriving in Indiana, Reuben set out again for Flint, Michigan. This time, he traveled alone—to a city where he knew no one—to begin the pursuit of his own vocational goals. This move began Reuben's successful 40-year career in the automobile industry. His career would take him to the halls of Harvard University and to the C-Suite of *Fortune* 500 companies worldwide, until he retired as the president of a major retailer and manufacturer of automobile materials.

Looking back on his success and his career, Reuben was unequivocal about two things. First, his affirmation that, "God was present, and His hand was all over so much of what happened in my life." And second, he also credited his own ability to shape his destiny through his hard work, confidence, competence, and his willingness to take risks. "I wasn't afraid of failure," Reuben told us. "I don't think you can be afraid of failure. I think that if you're afraid, you have trouble."

Reuben's story underscores the interconnectedness between each of the *Be Attitudes*. None of them operate in isolation. In Reuben's case, being Spirit-led prompted him to be bold and to take risks that he might not ordinarily have taken. According to Reuben, those early experiences defined his perception of how God moves in his life. They also cemented his decision to trust and follow the leading of the Spirit. His commitment to being Spirit-led was the guiding force from which Reuben drew on to take action to create and sustain wealth.

CHALLENGES TO BOLDNESS

Reuben's life in many ways paralleled our own. Reuben came from humble beginnings, was raised by a single mother, and traveled away from his place of birth for economic opportunity. The notable differences in our stories, beyond the fact that Reuben's life began in the American South in the 1960's is, of course, that he is a man. From speaking with him (and many of the other men that we interviewed), we could immediately tell that Reuben operated with a degree of self-confidence elusive to us.

Research shows men tend to be more confident in their abilities and spend less time considering the implications of failure than women.[8] This point is significant and mirrors our own experiences. We didn't decide who we would interview based on gender, and we gleaned valuable lessons from each of our interviewees. But both of us can recount times in our careers when a lack of confidence in our own abilities or ideas has held us back from pursuing a promotion or contributing fully in critical meetings. Some of the women spoke of familiar struggles with self-confidence because of their gender. But the good news is that these women did not stay stuck or limited. They continued to take charge of their futures and money!

The road to our preferred future is rarely easy. Whether the action is taken by a woman or man, stepping out from our current reality to the unknown can be downright frightening. Think about it. What do you think is the most common reason for *not* starting a new business, changing jobs, or accepting a challenging new role or assignment? Lack of money? Lack of time? Lack of support? All these reasons make sense and may account for some inaction in these areas. But when the layers of excuses are peeled back, we discover that in fact the real reason is fear. Fear in all its various forms is the primary challenger to *Be Bold*. Fear of rejection, fear of failure, and in some cases, even fear of success. We're sure you may have wrestled with some or all of these fear factors at some point in your life. As we'll discuss later in the chapter, while we won't be able to eradicate fear from our lives, we do need to understand and take actionable steps to *Be Bold* despite its presence. Let's begin that journey now.

Understanding Fear

As a society, we are getting better at talking about fear and owning up to the reality that we all experience fear as we strive for uncommon opportunities and richer rewards. Google the word *fear*, and you'll find a fairly antiseptic definition about a negative emotion caused by a sense that someone or something is dangerous. We're told it's a basic human emotion both innate and learned. Innate fear is linked to human biology. Perceived threats trigger fear from genetic codes naturally imprinted in our brain—the two most basic being the fear of falling and the fear of loud noises. Fear that is learned is highly individualized based on personal experiences, observations, and cues or lessons passed on from those around us. In all cases, fear is triggered by perceived harm to our mental, physical, or emotional well-being, regardless of whether the threat is real or imagined. Once triggered, our brain determines (based on our fight-or-flight response) whether we should confront the threat or flee for safety. The function of this powerful emotion is self-preservation and survival.

Science-based studies about fear have concluded that it is a natural, important, and necessary emotion meant to keep us safe and prevent us from making poor choices or attempting unreasonable and dangerous feats. But science doesn't tell the full story. A more comprehensive picture emerges when we view fear with a spiritual lens. The fact is that fear was not part of God's original plan for us. What science explains as a "natural" emotion was born unnaturally. We were not created with fear, and would not have felt it, apart from the fall of mankind. After Adam and Eve disobeyed and ate the fruit of the forbidden tree, the very first emotion they felt when God called out to them was the unfamiliar and gripping throes of fear. For them, and for us, fear is a byproduct of that original sin, and it marks our tragic separation from God, and the end of connection to our true selves as God had created us.

Fear is now an essential part of our DNA, designed to combat the dangers of this world, but identifying and managing it can be a challenge because of the adaptive and persistent nature of the emotion. It can be hidden or masked, but it doesn't go away. Fear can emerge suddenly, as an automatic, uninvited response, or mount up and overwhelm us after a sensible act of data gathering and examination. Let's say your more adventurous friend invites you to go skydiving, and without skipping a beat, you respond with a resounding no. Or perhaps you decline an invitation to address a crowd of hundreds because even the thought of standing in front of ten makes you ill. In both scenarios, fear can be easily identified as having a significant role in the decision. But fear in stealth mode can be difficult to pinpoint, especially for those gripped by the emotion.

Some of the most powerful triggers of our fears have been in place for a long time, perhaps since childhood. They camouflage, adapt, and blend in, so that many of us are not even aware we are acting out of fear. It may be hard to see that fear is holding us back from not starting or fulfilling desired lifelong goals. Even when fear is known and acknowledged, it's hard to get unstuck. The challenge with fear is its ability to smother dreams. Unless confronted and dealt with, the bitter root of fear will choke the very life from our dreams—leaving us broke, or at the very least, unfulfilled!

Whew! All of that sounds pretty grim, and having faced fear before, we knew we needed specific strategies to deal with its crippling force, as one of the biggest hindrances to our ability to *Be Bold*. Our interviewees did not disappoint. We left the conversations with these successful men and women feeling like we had just had a master class on how to deal with fear and approach new opportunities. From intentionally choosing unconventional careers to accepting challenging and risky assignments that everyone else had turned down, our interviewees took us to school on this *Be Attitude*.

The Ultimate Weapon against Fear

Pastor Mark, a minister in western New York, approaches ministry with a deep commitment to breaking down the barriers that keep people from getting closer to God. For him, this means holistically addressing a myriad of issues, including access to education, lack of single-family home ownership, health and wellness disparities, and economic empowerment. He also works tirelessly to inspire and create opportunities for the next generation of entrepreneurs and business leaders. From confrontations with neighborhood drug dealers to hardball negotiations with industry executives to mobilizing the community to challenge institutions and people perpetuating inequities, he's seen and done it all to make a difference within his community.

You can't be scared to do the type of work Pastor Mark is committed to and calling on others to follow. Yet he spoke candidly about the persistent nature of fear and doubt. He was also adamant about the effectiveness of combating fear at the source with the greatest weapon we have, which is the Word of God. "Faith is for the purpose of overcoming doubt," Pastor Mark told us. "Faith and doubt have to be in tension. But you read that Word, and that Word strengthens you, and that Word becomes a way of life."

Ephesians 6:17 describes the Bible as "the sword" of the Spirit, a powerful, offensive weapon against evil and anything that is not of God. This includes fear and other forms of deception liberally used by the devil. Fear amplifies the worst possible scenarios, focusing on the disaster that awaits us at every turn, especially if it involves change, action, and risk. So, while the Spirit seeks to guide our steps and decision-making to align with God's will, fear will do whatever it takes to prevent us from boldly moving forward to change or achieve. Here is the good news. We are on the winning side. Despite circumstances, or our own internal doubts, we have the power of the Spirit and the Word of God to overcome fear. As Pastor Mark shared, this power is activated when we internalize and choose to believe the Word of God. Here are a few of our favorite verses that we personalize and repeat to ourselves regularly:

- I can do all things through Christ who strengthens me. —Philippians 4:13

- If any of you lacks wisdom, let him ask of God, who gives to all liberally and without reproach, and it will be given to him. —James 1:5

- Yet in all these things we are more than conquerors through Him who loved us. —Romans 8:37

- For we are His workmanship, created in Christ Jesus for good works, which God prepared beforehand that we should walk in them. —Ephesians 2:10

- Do you see a man who excels in his work? He will stand before kings; He will not stand before unknown men. —Proverbs 22:29

As believers in Christ, in the face of doubt and fear, especially insecurities about our own personal abilities, we can be assured that Scripture has already provided encouragement. We can be confident that God will provide the strength to achieve and to persist.

DO IT SCARED

Anna, who we met in chapter 2, had no aspirations of becoming a successful business owner. Less than fifteen years ago, she was a self-described "regular employee," content to keep her head down and do her job. Her life changed when, in conversation with her employer, she realized he did not have a solid plan to safeguard the future of the business. "Boy, did that wake me up," Anna stated. "My livelihood could be on the line because this person was being nonchalant," she told us. Shortly after that realization, another casual conversation with a longtime business vendor turned into a surprise offer of co-ownership in his company. With no training in business, she was initially reluctant to accept the offer, based on what she described as her risk-avoidant personality, and her inability to see her own worth. Looking back at that time she said, "I was extremely nervous, but my husband, who's also an engineer, is the total opposite. He doesn't mind the risk. He's like, 'Go for it. I know you can do it. Go ahead. I have your back.'" Anna noted, "I didn't recognize my worth at first. Someone had to tell me I was worthy for me to then say, 'Oh, wow. He's right.' And it's not out of arrogance I'm saying that, but I had to think about what my role was, and what I brought to the table, compared to other people."

In the end, Anna pushed past her fears and doubt, armed with a recognition of her worth, her ability, and her potential. Today, she is the co-owner of a multi-million-dollar engineering firm with over one hundred and fifty employees. Anna was able to change her life and that of her family because she was able to embody *Be Bold*. In Anna's case, she didn't begin "feeling" like an entrepreneur. In her mind, she was a technical engineer, a good worker whose labor was meant to make someone else rich. While Anna lived under that false perception, her potential to successfully run her own company was clearly visible to those around her. Her act of boldness started with recognizing her own value and acting on that truth.

The popular phrase, "do it scared," now immortalized on t-shirts, Instagram hashtags, and book titles, has become a motivational mantra for the masses. Its universal appeal highlights that everyone, at some point, will be faced with fear, when what is needed most is action. The "it" in the phrase is irrelevant. The point of the statement is to deliberately choose to act toward the realization of dreams and goals, despite being afraid.

RECOGNIZING OUR TRUE POTENTIAL

In 2020, after a few months of being quarantined during the global pandemic caused by COVID-19, a set of fascinating before-and-after pictures began circulating on the internet. These pictures showed remarkable improvements in air quality in different cities around the world. Places like New York City, New Delhi, London, and Moscow were dramatically captured with clear air and blue skies, instead of the usual smog and haze caused by pollution. The pictures were a peek into the unspoiled, natural beauty of these cities. We wondered how these city residents felt seeing the purity of their surroundings for what could have been their first time.

These photos also made us reflect on the similarities to our own lives. When we live below our true potential, below what God has for us, it shows. Too many of us plod along in a gray and smoggy existence of falsehoods, including false security, false comfort, and a false perception of our aptitude and ability. The illusion created by fear is not true even if it is familiar. What may feel like comfort and safety is no more than a fear-based illusion obscuring the truth of our potential for growth, success, and true fulfillment. The identity we take on, and the labels we give ourselves, may become normal for us, and for those around us. But normal is not what God has in store, and it is a poor substitute for the truth. The truth is that we are extraordinary! We were created as masterpieces to reflect God's glory! When we act with boldness, we are choosing to live fully in the very best personal version of ourselves, as designed by God.

AMBITION IS NOT A DIRTY WORD

Fear is not the only culprit that undermines our ability to act. Wayne, an expert on faith and achievement, whose wisdom on viewing money rightly we shared in chapter 1, believes another issue could be a lack of ambition that was perpetuated by faulty teaching in the church. "When I was in seminary, they actually had a book I had to read that castigated people who had ambitions, and made these people feel bad, because the Scripture talks about 'selfish ambition'" (see Philippians 2:3). He described the ill effects of this thinking as, "So many Christians settle because they feel, 'Well, I don't want to be too ambitious, I don't want to be too pushy, I don't want to be [fill in the blank].'" Wayne told us, "And God will give you the desires of your heart. You're saying to God, 'Well, I ain't got no desires, I'll take whatever You give me.'" We could feel Wayne's desire to inspire change when he exclaimed with passion: "No! What are your goals? We have to start thinking bigger!"

Ouch! The interview with Wayne struck a nerve for both of us. Studying our own lives, we could see instances of how our own desires to stay comfortable led to complacency and stagnation. While there is nothing wrong with the desire to be safe or comfortable, we have to be careful that, in these states, we're not being stunted. Growth is most often achieved when we are stretched and challenged, neither of which is comfortable.

Our interview with Ralph, the first African American to become vice president in the advertising division of AT&T, a *Fortune* 500 company, and the recipient of the company's highest honor (the CEO Circle of Excellence award), provided us with an apt illustration of bold ambition at its finest. Ralph, now retired, pursued his career with a level of boldness we found awe-inspiring. Early in his career he began having proactive meetings with his senior leadership to learn from them and to share his aspirations. "So, I learned early on that we are so often limited and we are so often set back because we use 'I didn't know,' or 'I didn't have access to this,' or 'This was not made available to me' as excuses," Ralph told us. He asked, "Well, what steps did you take to gain some of this knowledge and gain some of this opportunity, you know? Did you put yourself out there? Did you ever talk to anybody about your career aspirations?" Despite this positive outlook, Ralph was quick to point out that his climb up the corporate ladder was far from easy. "I mean, there were plenty of setbacks, but I viewed them as opportunities to show how the Lord could use me," Ralph shared. "I never got disrespectful, I never showed fear or anger. I was so blessed to have a village around me of people who had my back and who said, 'Hey, I see how hard you're working. I want to help you do this and do this,' because you don't get through the big jobs like that by yourself."

Ralph gave us further insight into his story by candidly sharing how he overcame career disappointment through bold action that eventually changed the course of his life. After being passed over for several promotions, a frustrated Ralph called his corporate office to move his retirement account in preparation for quitting. The woman who answered the phone, a stranger to Ralph, challenged him on his decision. She said, "Ralph, you've been at AT&T for all these years. Just because something doesn't go your way, you're just going to quit?" Ralph thought she was unaware of the struggles he faced on the job and responded by citing the discrimination and bias he experienced at the company. But the woman on the phone was undeterred. "Okay. You told me you are a man of faith. Where's your faith? If the path is already paved, you don't need any faith." She said, "Let me tell you, young man. You're too young to quit on yourself. Hang in there because there will be other opportunities."

Ralph decided then and there to stay with the company. Shortly after that encounter, he was invited to interview to be regional manager for the state of California. This role was tough and high profile. Although skeptical about actually getting the job, Ralph took the interview but warned his wife he was unlikely to get the role. I said, "You know what? We're gonna go to Los Angeles for this interview because it gives us a free weekend in California. They're going to pay for everything, but there's no way I'm going to get this job." The vice president who interviewed Ralph told him every reason why he should not take the job: it was a challenging market, it had an extremely diverse employee team, California was considered a "sue happy" state—the list went on. But Ralph grew more excited. "I thought, this is my kind of job, you know? Because if I can master this, I set myself on a course for bigger things at AT&T. And I knew everybody was going to be watching Los Angeles. It was our third largest market," he remembered. At the end of the interview, Ralph was asked if he was willing to accept the challenge. He boldly replied, "Absolutely. I don't think you have a better candidate than me."

Ralph got the job, but the challenges did not end with this good news. "When I started the new job, my director told me on my very first day in his office, 'I didn't pick you. I didn't select you. The vice president told me I had to take you, and I don't believe you can do this job. So, I'm just going to wait for you to fail.'" After this unsolicited rant, Ralph replied, "You know what? I appreciate your honesty. But you know, the chapter hasn't been written yet, and you don't get to write my chapter." A mere two years later, Ralph was the number one ranked manager in that area, and he held that ranking for five successive years. Ambition was not the only element in Ralph's success, but it was an important part. He set audacious goals for himself and pursued them with the boldness of a man who understood that ambition is not a dirty word.

As inspiring as we found Ralph's story, as women, we were thrilled to see similar boldness in another woman, Jenna, who is now the CEO of a marketing and IT firm and was unabashed about her ambition to be successful. "When I was with Gillette and with Johnson & Johnson, very quickly I was like, 'Okay, where's the top? Because that's where I'm heading,'" she said, with a laugh. Jenna's early commitment to ambitious goal setting continues to help her achieve as a business owner. "So, if I could do this on the biggest stage—I mean, these were *Fortune* 500 companies—if I could do this on the biggest stage, this is what I can do. So, when I had my own company, I saw no reason why the product or the services that were provided would be any less than excellent. Gillette was paying me to do their most excellent work. And it's not like all of a sudden those talents diminish because I have my own company. I can produce the best of the best … world-class stuff."

BOLD IS NOT ALWAYS BIG

James Clear, in his groundbreaking book *Atomic Habits*, writes, "Every action you take is a vote for the type of person you wish to become. No single instance will transform your beliefs, but as the votes build up, so does the evidence of your new identity. This is one reason why meaningful change does not require radical change. Small habits can make a meaningful difference by providing evidence of a new identity."[9] Being bold is not always about big moves. Every decision does not have to be monumental. You don't have to be moving to a new city or starting a company. Develop the practice of reliable action, the practice of fully showing up, and the practice of shining consistently.

Think back to Anna's story. Although we highlighted her decision to become the co-owner of a company as her bold move, Anna was being bold prior to that decision. Her consistent action yielded results: she worked hard and displayed excellence right where she was planted, even before she became a business owner. Saying yes to being the project lead for a challenging assignment and completing it with excellence, applying for a promotion or a new job, despite self-sabotaging ideas of not being qualified, finally making an appointment to meet with a financial counselor to develop and stick with a budget, or making a commitment to networking with someone unknown to you, despite being an introvert are all examples of small but bold moves that over time can build up confidence and can lead to bigger leaps and more opportunities to shine.

Blessed are the bold, for they shall
realize success beyond their dreams.

In this chapter, we challenged ourselves to *Be Bold*, which includes taking risks, being confident and courageous, acting in the face of fear, and shining brilliantly. Being bold requires that we set ambitious goals and take risks based on an accurate picture of ourselves. It's also about refusing to live a "less-than" life: one that is less than our potential, and how we are created by God.

BE PRAYERFUL

Father, help me to step boldly into the path You have ordained for me. Help me to act in the face of any fear or doubt I may feel, knowing You promised to strengthen me. Help me to see myself as You see me, and to take consistent action based on that truth. Help me to not get complacent or stagnant but to continue with forward progress toward my goals. Amen.

BE DOERS

1. Identify something God is calling you to but you have been afraid to pursue.

2. Assess whether there is a part of your personality you are dimming for fear of being in the spotlight. Begin to express your true self.

3. What initial step can you take toward your financial goals, despite the nervous feelings you may have? Take bold action.

Chapter 5

BE INTENTIONAL

Blessed are the intentional,
for they shall accomplish their goals.

Shortly after developing the primary framework for this book, we were invited to teach a Bible study class. Minutes into the class, the atmosphere became uncomfortable and still after we asked a question of the audience. No one spoke and blank faces stared back at us. Finally, one brave soul raised his hand, and slowly a few more inched up. What had we done to cause such a reaction? What could possibly have left seasoned saints of God unsure and reluctant to literally show their hand? Had we asked them to publicly confess a sin or to find the exact chapter and verse of some obscure biblical figure? No, we hadn't done either of those things. What we had done was ask this small group of believers whether any of them aspired to be wealthy.

Maybe some were taken aback by the pointedness of the question, but for the majority, we knew it was more than that. We knew because at various points in our own lives, we had the same reaction.

After the initial shock and half-hearted hand raises, people began to provide the following explanations: "I don't want to be rich. I just want to be comfortable." "I just want to help people. I don't think about money." "I try not to concern myself about money. I just want to be satisfied with what I have."

While agreeing that having money was important, the group wasn't ready to go so far as admitting that getting rich should be, much less was, a goal. They seemed to be really uncomfortable with the question, and we heard the skepticism and uncertainty in the voices of the few who replied. As the night progressed, we heard admirable stories of sacrifice. We heard testimonies of mothers and grandmothers who fed entire neighborhoods and took food from the mouths of their own children to give to someone else in need. Tale after tale of sacrifice, of giving, of serving, despite the struggle to stay one step away from persistent bills, family obligations, and debt were recounted as badges of honor. But no one wanted to claim a desire to be rich.

We don't know how many in the crowd were convinced that night, nor how many people will be convinced after reading this book, but discussions surrounding aspirations for wealth are worth having. If we are to have the kind of impact that is needed, both individually and as a community, this conversation is vital. Before we can truly explore the how-to of getting rich, as noted in the book's title, we must first determine whether it's okay to be rich, or said another way, whether it's permissible to seek wealth as believers.

We asked the Bible study attendees what they would do if money were no object. We asked them to dream. As we did this, people settled in, and the tension decreased a little. This was more familiar and safe ground. Some of the stories changed. Some turned into ambitious goals of starting hospitals, funding schools, taking missions trips across the world, and caring for family and neighbors. This invitation to dream highlighted something important. If we are to realize some of the God-sized dreams in our hearts, dreams that require large investments of money, something has to change.

CHANGE REQUIRES ACTION

At one point in Cassandra's career she found herself bored, stagnant, and stuck in an unfulfilling job. She desperately wanted a change but there were no signs of relief. And guess what? Nothing changed. She described it as living in an endless loop of the same day, as portrayed in the 1993 movie *Groundhog Day*. She woke each day and made the same commute to the same job. She prayed and asked God for a change, and ... nothing changed. She went through a whole host of emotions and wasted lots of time, until one day it finally sunk in. Nothing was going to change until she took action. She had to move beyond staring out her office window, lost in daydreams of what her reality could be. Dreaming is wonderful. It is the essential starting point of achieving our goals. Dreaming gives us something to look forward to, and in that sense, it gives us purpose. But it's not enough to have a dream. We must move beyond dreaming to setting goals, making plans, and taking action to achieve them. This is the process that finally yielded the change Cassandra desired in her career. The same principle of taking action that applies to finding career or vocational fulfillment applies to our money.

Why do we leave our financial well-being to chance? Why do so many of us take such a haphazard attitude toward something so important? Is such an important topic not worth the utmost consideration, research, education, planning, and execution? These actions

Haphazardly created or inconsistently applied plans will undermine our ability to take effective action toward our goals.

are all components of the next two chapters: *Be Intentional* and *Be Diligent*. Each one is an important step in achieving our goals. They involve an act of our will, a conscious decision to do something specific. They embody what it means to live on purpose.

Be Intentional is how we maintain the focus and connection between our mindset, actions, and goals. It is the opposite of failing to plan, floating along the sea of life, being solely reactionary, and accepting whatever comes our way. Haphazardly created or inconsistently applied plans will undermine our ability to take effective action toward our goals. Our success and best results are achieved by both an intentional mindset, and an intentional process for taking action. None of the spiritually grounded habits of mind that we covered in previous chapters can be done on autopilot. We must embrace a right-minded view of God, and an esteemed view of our potential to achieve and create wealth. We also need to submit to the will of the Lord in our decision-making and summon courage to act in the midst of fear. All of these actions require continuous, if not daily, renewal. *Be Intentional* is a rejection of a set-it-and-forget-it manner of living. *Be Intentional* underscores the critical need for us to decisively and deliberately attune our moral compass to live according to our values.

We asked Miles, the first person we interviewed, if becoming wealthy was a deliberate goal for him. "Yes! Absolutely deliberate," Miles stated. The question was posed to all of our participants, but the most emphatic answer was from Miles. He answered without hesitation—almost before the question was fully formed, leaving us momentarily at a loss for words. Although we made the inquiry, we didn't expect such a forthright answer. We were accustomed to people, particularly Christians, denying, hesitating, or giving lengthy qualifying answers to explain why wealth attainment was, or more accurately, was not, one of their goals. It's no wonder then, that we were surprised by Miles's unabashed reply that wealth building was one of his goals. He followed up with, "It still is. I'm not ten percent of the way there."

Miles is a CEO, renowned musician, entrepreneur, and author. His products are in major retail stores across the United States, and his music is streamed around the globe. Most of his wealth has been attained through intellectual property licensing and royalties. Although he is busy with his business dealings and high-demand performances, we first became acquainted with him because of his work to motivate and inspire youth in the foster care system. Miles's track record of business and financial success, paired with his actions to improve the lives of others, embodied many of our own goals. This early conversation with Miles was one of several that were key to identifying our next *Be Attitude, Be Intentional*. Even with all that Miles had achieved, he still articulated clear goals for his future. Moreover, as we would later learn, he deliberately pursued his goals with a well-honed process of planning, action, and reflection. Simply put, Miles's success was fueled by his ability to *Be Intentional*.

As mentioned above, one of the questions we asked our participants was whether becoming wealthy was a deliberate goal. We received different responses from the group. Some replied in the affirmative, others noted that the goal was to avoid the lack they experienced growing up. A few defined the objective as seeking financial security, and rejected labels such as rich or wealthy. However they defined their goal, our interviewees all went about achieving their stated goal in a similar manner. Namely, they took personal responsibility to decide what they wanted out of life (whether it was to become wealthy, escape poverty, secure a certain standard of living for their families, or have a specific amount of money in the bank), they figured out what it would take to get them there, they planned accordingly, and worked hard to execute their plans. Despite the varying definitions and goals, everyone had long-term financial objectives. Additionally, each of them expressed a drive toward values and the service of others that prioritized those goals over the attainment of wealth.

THE PROCESS

Most people do not associate the memory of waking up to the aroma of breakfast cooking on a Saturday morning with hitting rock bottom on one of their lowest days, but Keith does. Today, Keith is the successful owner of a thriving dental practice in upstate New York, but staring over the precipice of financial ruin was an experience he has not forgotten. He describes his early dental school days as among the lowest moments of his life. As a young dental student, he was broke. He, his wife, and his daughter were almost out of food and close to being evicted from their apartment. "We were literally going from paycheck to paycheck, and whatever we needed to buy, we just bought, but we never really looked at the future," Keith shared. One day, they were down to their last supply of food—a can of tuna fish and one egg they were saving for their daughter. Keith's brother-in-law was visiting at the time. On that fateful Saturday morning, Keith woke up to the smell of his brother-in-law frying up that last egg, and as he says, "I lost it. I went ballistic on him for frying up that egg…And it was at that time that the Holy Spirit said, 'Okay, so when are you going to trust in me? You're trying to do everything on your own. When are you going to trust in me?'" That event was a turning point in Keith's life. He decided then that drastic change was needed, beginning with creating a plan. Keith's story from that point forward modeled the process of intentional living. In the section that follows, we will review each of these steps in turn: identify what you want to achieve, write it down, make a plan, and adjust as necessary. In other words, *Be Intentional.*

Identify What You Want to Achieve

We can start identifying what we want to achieve by asking ourselves similar questions to what Keith had:

- What do I want my life to look like?

- Where do I want to live?

- How much money would I like to give to worthy causes?

- How long will it take me to pay off all my debt?

- How much money will it take me to live comfortably in retirement?

- What kind of inheritance would I like to leave my children?

We cannot write the vision if we don't first have the vision. Having a vision, or the process of setting goals, harnesses the power of our dreams. The sky's the limit when it comes to dreaming. The above questions, and others, ground us in setting specific goals. Additional planning is also protection against uncertainties in life and unexpected setbacks. Even if you want to be financially secure, as opposed to wealthy, like a few of the individuals we interviewed, the process begins with goal setting. No matter how you define financial security, success relies on setting goals. There has to be a target at which you are aiming.

Begin with the end in mind. Entrepreneur and author Seth Godin has been quoted as saying, "The thing about goals is that living without them is a lot more fun, in the short run. It seems to me, though, that the people who get things done, who lead, who grow and who make an impact ... those people have goals."[10]

Gina, whose tithing and investing stories we shared with you in chapter two, felt like her status as a "double minority" impacted her salary throughout her working life. During our interview, she reflected, "Looking back on it, every job I've ever had, I have always gotten paid less than the comparable White male next to me." She knew that in order to have the life she wanted, she would have to do more than just collect a regular salary. She has built her wealth over time by carefully and diligently saving and investing, but it all began with her setting a goal. She began with the end in mind, and a lot followed, including some setbacks caused by unwise investments that didn't yield good returns, but her journey to success began with this specific, clearly articulated goal.

The reality of what it actually takes to achieve our goals can sap the excitement and enthusiasm from our pursuits. It's normal to get discouraged. Here are several tips to stay the course:

- Remember your "why" and revisit the values and goals you are working toward for motivation and encouragement.

- Break down large tasks into smaller, manageable pieces. Start tackling goals one at a time. Do one thing at a time, and cross items off your list as they are completed.

- Continue to trust God.

God allows us to share in the act of creating our preferred future. Taking personal responsibility and establishing plans is an important aspect of our faith orientation to allow God to order our steps. In fact, we are creating the conditions for the working of the Spirit to open doors and to create opportunities. God is sovereign, but we should also plan. The Scriptures show that God works in the midst of plans.

Write It Down

Now that you have a goal in mind, it's important to write it down. Create a physical record of what you want to accomplish. Once again, the Bible is instructive on this topic. First, Habakkuk 2:2 instructs us to write the vision and make it plain, so that those who see it will run with it. In addition, in Luke 14:28–30, Jesus asks, "For which of you, intending to build a tower, does not sit down first and count the cost, whether he has enough to finish it— lest, after he has laid the foundation, and is not able to finish, all who see it begin to mock him saying, 'This man began to build and was not able to finish.'"

Even before you chart the ins and outs of getting to your destination, writing the destination down, or having a picture of it that you look at regularly, will make it more real to you. Your goal is more likely to remain a dream if it remains in your head. Set it before your eyes. If possible, put it in a place where you'll see it often. At the very least, take it out of its storage place and read it frequently. This serves as a reminder of your goals. It helps to keep you accountable. It will spur you on.

Science supports the Bible's instruction to create a written record of your goals. A study reported in *Forbes* showed that "vividly describing your goals in written form is strongly associated with goal success, and people who very vividly describe or picture their goals are anywhere from 1.2 to 1.4 times more likely to successfully accomplish their goals than people who don't."[11] There are two scientific explanations as to why this is the case, both of which we have stated before. First, writing something down creates a visual record to which we can frequently refer, which of course leads to increased likelihood that we'll remember it. Second, we are more likely to remember something we've written ourselves, as opposed to something we've just heard. Another study done by Dr. Gail Matthews, a psychology professor at the Dominican University of California, showed that participants who wrote down their goals were significantly more likely to accomplish them than those who did not. Overall, the study showed that people are thirty-three percent more likely to achieve their goals if they write them down daily.[12]

That's part of the popularity of vision boards. These visual records of what people want to achieve, either short or long term, can be as simple as having pictures representing the desired item or ideal, or as involved as a description of the specific dream or goal. Creating vision boards is a common activity at the beginning of the year, when people are making New Year's resolutions or otherwise planning for the year ahead. However, just like New Year's resolutions, they can be ineffective and quickly abandoned if they are not appropriately paired with other steps that build in accountability and action. We've been to many vision board parties where the gathering was just that: a party where the creation of the board is simply a cover for groups to eat, drink, and socialize. To be effective, a vision board, or any written documentation of the goal, must be accompanied by a plan.

Make a Plan

Now that you have a documented picture of what you want to achieve, how are you going to get there? It's time to create a plan. After Keith and his wife settled on the vision for their lives, they took the critical step of creating a plan for the future. Their plan tackled a range of issues like debt, cashflow, and savings. They also considered what resources they had at their disposal, where they needed more information and knowledge, and how their financial standing could change over time. We should make the same types of assessments in building our plans. Key considerations include understanding our goals, our current financial situation, and the timeline or milestones that will mark our progress. Questions that can guide this process include:

- What is it going to take to get me to where I want to go?

- Do I need to go back to school?

- Are there free resources available or will it require a financial commitment?

- Are there strategic relationships or partnerships I need to seek out?

There are several reasons why people struggle with following through with their plans, but one of the main ones may be the seeming enormity of all that needs to be done. Looking at the big picture and all that has to happen in order to get from point A to point B can be overwhelming. This is the lesson in Jesus's story about counting the cost before starting to build. Achieving our goals may require multiple levels of plans, some drilling down with more specificity in key areas, or tracking different timelines for short- and long-term goals. For example, under the broad plan for achieving financial security, there may be subplans for retirement, debt reduction, investment, and/or diversifying income.

Adjust as Necessary

Look at your plan from time to time to see where you are. Don't be afraid to make adjustments if necessary. Maybe your goals have changed. Maybe the steps you outlined before have to be adjusted because of life circumstances. Maybe the tools you chose just aren't working. Don't use these events as excuses to get discouraged or to give up. Make an honest assessment of where you are, see what's working and what's not, make the necessary adjustments, and keep moving.

Blessed are the intentional,
for they shall accomplish their goals.

Be Intentional is our personal stance against the common pitfall of living life on autopilot. This *Be Attitude* challenges us to take personal responsibility for clarifying our goals, creating informed and realistic plans for success, and consciously assessing and making revisions as needed.

BE PRAYERFUL

God, I don't want to be aimlessly afloat on the sea of life. Help me be intentional in the decisions I make, and the steps I take, to make my dreams a reality. Amen.

BE DOERS

1. Think about, then write down, what you want your financial life to look like five years from now.

2. What steps do you need to take to make this happen?

3. Are there additional resources needed?

Chapter 6

BE DILIGENT

*Blessed are the diligent, for they shall
enjoy the fruits of their labor.*

A few years ago, we took a detour from writing this book to take a group of teenage students enrolled in our church's Academy on an enrichment program to Belize. The program was designed to introduce science and technology concepts, integrated with music and the arts, to Belizean middle school students. In turn, the U.S. students who traveled with us received cultural enrichment and leadership development training to serve as camp counselors. Cassandra and the leadership team of the Academy had the vision of impacting the lives of young people in the church and the surrounding community. Making plans to do so was not enough. We needed to establish connections with the host country, raise funds, train students and adult teachers, select and prepare curriculum, gather and ship resources, and secure hotel and ground transportation for the team. We could go into greater detail about all that was required to make the trip happen, but we're sure you get the idea. The bottom line is that to get all this accomplished, everyone involved had to be diligent.

Be Diligent picks up where *Be Intentional* leaves off. It is the next step in the process. A step without which, all the prior actions would be pointless. To write down your vision and create the perfect plan to achieve it but then *do* nothing (or even do something half-heartedly) is akin to not having a plan at all. Some people might be great at conceptualizing a successful future for themselves, but they fail to follow through to make it happen. They can see the big picture, but they're not so good at breaking things down into smaller steps and figuring out what's necessary to bring the picture into focus. Others may be great at goal setting and may even get as far as the planning stage, but then get stalled in the execution stage. To *Be Diligent* is to follow through with each step of the journey to success.

David, an accomplished leadership expert and successful CEO who we interviewed, credits his father with teaching him a valuable lesson about diligence when he was just a boy. "Success is not a birthright," David's father said. "You have to go out and earn it." Another strong influence in David's life was his grandfather, who prayed over him, and accurately declared that he would be the first millionaire in their family. David grew up in an athletic family that reinforced a strong work ethic. His grandfather was a preacher and a coach. His father was a retired college football coach. To say that these two men instilled the value of discipline in David is an understatement. One of the many lessons he learned from them was that a person can have any dream he or she wants, but they have to be willing to put in the time, effort, and energy to go out and make that dream a reality.

Besides the influence of these close family members, David also remembers that from an early age he was surrounded by hardworking and persistent individuals. As the son and grandson of coaches, he was exposed to athletes who "wanted to go to the NFL…who were dreamers, hard workers, grinders—people who were spending ten, twenty hours a week on their craft." Making it in the big leagues was probably a childhood dream for many of these athletes. They probably had heroes of their own who they emulated, and whose success they wanted to model. These athletes knew, as David's grandfather and father did, that without hard work, their dreams would remain just that—dreams. So, they became the models David and others would look up to. They were people who were not about excuses, and were accomplishing feats that were both physically and mentally challenging. Their hard work reinforced the message that David was being taught at home.

This same message of consistent effort and hard work lies at the heart of *Be Diligent*. However, instead of brute strength or mindless endurance, the fascinating men and women we interviewed showed us that *Be Diligent* refers to our capacity to work sensibly and strategically toward wealth building in full alignment with our values and long-term priorities. *Be Diligent* summarizes the necessary "tough-love" points of our discussion, including setting boundaries, committing to learning and personal growth, and making wise, disciplined choices with our money.

"GET RICH QUICK" IS A MYTH

Social media thrives on telling the stories of outliers. Headlines such as *How I Quit My Corporate Job and Became a Millionaire in Six Months,* or *Woman Turns $50 Idea into Million-Dollar Company Working Just 4 Hours a Week,* are all too common nowadays. Viral headlines like these peddle the idea that riches can be gained in a matter of weeks or months with little to no effort. Some of these stories are amplifying the experiences of just a few outliers. Unfortunately, most are, at best, overblown distortions of reality, and at worst, pure fiction.

There is seldom such a thing as overnight success. Businesspeople, athletes, and everyday success stories have given account of how they worked hard behind the scenes for years, enduring rejection and failures, doing things that may be considered drudgery, only to eventually make it big and have people assume their success happened overnight. While so-called overnight success stories do occur—after all, we serve a God for whom nothing is impossible—the reality for most of us is that achieving success will take time and consistent personal effort.

Why Can't God Supernaturally Make Me Rich?

This chapter's emphasis on the role of personal responsibility and our own sweat equity in wealth building is an acknowledgment that we are in partnership with the Lord. As we consider God's promises to bless us and to prosper the work of our hands, we get excited, and rightly so! After all, God is the ultimate promise keeper. Everything He does, all His gifts, are motivated by His great love for us and His character trait of being good, as we discussed in chapter 1. All we have to do is receive His goodness and be thankful.

But does this absolve us from all responsibility for our own success? Do we then just pray to God for financial success and wait for money to fall into our laps? These may sound like ridiculous questions. The reply of most people would be, "of course not!" But in reality, many of us have the tendency to do just that. We often miss a part of the equation. We treat God's promises as if they're wish-upon-a-star concepts. If we just believe hard enough . . . If we just confess

Your diligent steps, no matter how small, will create momentum toward realizing your dreams.

it enough times ... If we call it in, it will just come to us. Nothing could be further from the truth. Success, financial and otherwise, requires our capacity to be diligent. We cannot stress this enough: the promise above that God will bless the work of our hands means our hands should be working! If we don't work, there's nothing for Him to bless. Proverbs 10:4 tells us lazy hands make for poverty, but diligent hands bring wealth.

EMBRACE A MEASURED
APPROACH TO WEALTH BUILDING

Think about the financial goals you identified with our last *Be Attitude, Be Intentional.* Remembering your "why" while being diligent about pursuing those goals will both drive you toward continued progress and protect against disappointment. Slow and steady progress is still progress. Your diligent steps, no matter how small, will create momentum toward realizing your dreams. It takes most entrepreneurs over three years for their business to be profitable, and seven to ten years before their business can be deemed a success. Individuals who diligently save, make investments, and spend wisely will increase their net worth.

Pastor Malcolm, from chapter two, shared how his measured approach to wealth building serves to protect his investment. He advised, "I've come to appreciate [that] the discipline of business will serve to your benefit. So, if there's a deal that seems too good to be true and it's not going through the proper process, I tend to walk away because I've discovered the process will protect me. And when I jump the process, that's when I tend to get in trouble. So, I've learned to pursue opportunities, but in a more disciplined manner.

I think that is something extremely important, particularly for people who are desiring to build their wealth. Fast money generally ends in heartbreak."

Being disciplined in managing our finances is easier if we learn some strategies, and it has never been easier to do so. There are a host of financial management models, frameworks, and books that will break down specific steps and tout a particular brand of managing money. The best one is the one that is right for you—one that you will follow, and most importantly, one that follows biblical principles.

After years of successfully building his wealth portfolio, and coaching others to do the same, Reuben, the automobile executive whose story we featured in *Be Bold*, was eager to share a host of valuable advice. Reuben's suggestions—twelve to be exact—underscore the diligence necessary to achieve success. Among the top things he advised was this: "From my standpoint, I don't believe in get-rich-quick schemes. I think it requires hard work... I really believe that's very important."

So, what's the bottom line? Do your own research, consider your own circumstances and priorities, and resolve to diligently follow a long-view perspective on wealth attainment that includes a firm understanding that wealth can be achieved by taking personal responsibility for lifestyle choices, money management, and smart spending habits.

You Can *Learn to Build Wealth*

A consistent trait among the wealthy individuals we interviewed was their financial literacy and their confidence in their ability to learn and grow. For sure, not all of them started that way. However, in each of their stories was a belief that they had what it took to gain the skills or knowledge to meet their goals. For them, the issue wasn't whether they were fully equipped at the moment. Many shared stories of having to gain new knowledge to capitalize on different opportunities, but this didn't stop them because they were attuned to the future and optimistic about their chances for success.

Motivational speaker and business leader Wayne shared, "I'm a lifelong student. And I believe the great ones are always lifelong students—constantly learning more. Like I said, I went back to school in my fifties [to complete] my doctorate." Wayne also noted, "Because I knew there was more work on me that I had to do, I took a year off from speaking—writing papers and going back to the library—to grow. Even now, today, I've had my doctorate for a number of years now, but I'm still growing me, I'm still learning how to become better at creating wealth."

Now, let's be clear. You do not need a PhD to discover the ins and outs of wealth building. We're big fans of education and have two terminal degrees between us. However, our formal education did not adequately prepare us for managing or growing our money. As a matter of fact, it's this gap in our knowledge that drove us to begin the journey of researching and writing this book. The majority of people who become wealthy do not have degrees in finance. Among the people we interviewed, not one of them did.

Wealth is not reserved for people in a particular field or in a particular area, as we've already discussed. Some people make money by working for companies their entire lives. Others are entrepreneurial by nature and start their own companies at an early age. Some people exhibit both tendencies and have done both. Likewise, wealth is not just for those who are born with particular talents or smarts. Pastor Malcolm notes, "I think there's some people who, like in every other field, have a natural gifting. They're gifted to make money. But I think most people who are not born with it make decisions to develop this discipline." First and foremost among these decisions is to develop financial literacy.

Developing Financial Literacy

If you're an adult intent on building wealth, you need to understand the basics of financial literacy. This can't be outsourced to a financial planner or left up to a spouse, parent, or any other individual. You need to take personal responsibility for your own financial education. This doesn't mean you don't need expert guidance or can't make financial decisions in partnership with a loved one or business associates. However, without the basic knowledge, you will exclude yourself from active participation in critical decisions that will impact your future.

The major topics of financial literacy vary depending on the source (some sources include identity and fraud protection as well as utilizing credit). However, most sources include the following:

1. Generating Income

2. Budgeting and Spending

3. Avoiding Debt

4. Saving

5. Investing

6. Taxes and Insurance

Some of you may have noticed an important omission in the above list of popular financial literacy topics: tithing. We discussed the centrality of the tithe in chapter 1, so we won't go in depth here. However, the importance of tithing cannot be overstated. Returning a tenth portion of our earnings to the Lord should be done first, before progressing to any further allocations.

Whether you are an entrepreneur or an employee, gaining knowledge of personal finance in these six areas will help you take charge of your finances and make better decisions about your money. As your knowledge grows, so will your ability to take advantage of different opportunities. According to Pastor Malcolm: "I think [one needs] to respect wealth and business as its own discipline. So, in the same way an individual may have a library of ... whatever their given hobby is, if you want to build wealth, you should study it. You should study it as any other field of discipline. So, for years I have read financial newspapers, financial periodicals, and books [and attended] seminars. And I think that's where a lot of folks miss an opportunity." He concluded by offering the following advice: "It just means that every day you want to get up and read the financial section. And don't ignore it when the Wall Street snippet comes up on the news. Those are things you actually want to start paying attention to. And you rarely will find a businessperson who doesn't want to talk about their business. And so, by actively developing your own financial library, you will increase your literacy, and you will start to see opportunities where otherwise they would've been invisible."

Anna, now the co-owner of an engineering company, recognized that she didn't have the requisite business knowledge to run a company when she was first offered the partnership. As an engineer, she was very confident in her technical abilities, but confessed she had a lot to learn about running a business. "I wish that, even though I'm a technical person, they would have encouraged us to maybe take more business courses, or to be more well-rounded in that area because being an entrepreneur, starting a company, it isn't just putting a name on the door." Anna prioritized learning on the job about operating agreements, financial statements and evaluations, taxes, benefits, and payroll, and she credits her business partner, who has more business acumen, with balancing her skill set.

Know When to Seek Out Expert Advice

Self-directed learning has great value, but it also has its limits. One must know when they've reached this limit and seek expert advice to take them the rest of the way. The Bible has a lot to say about the value of wise counsel. The following verses come to mind: "Where there is no counsel, the people fall; but in the multitude of counselors there is safety" (Proverbs 11:14). "Without counsel, plans go awry, but in the multitude of counselors they are established" (Proverbs 15:22). "A wise man will hear and increase learning, and a man of understanding will attain wise counsel" (Proverbs 1:5). These are but some of the truths that Proverbs teaches.

Anna did not depend solely on self-directed learning and learning on the job. She also sought out experts to help her and her family achieve their financial goals. She recounted, "I think it was valuable, and we still have financial advisors to give us a perspective of what we need to have to meet our financial goals—trusted professionals. I don't have an MBA. I'm not a wealth manager, but you hire people who can do that for you. And I think you should find the people who match what your goals are."

Making Small Sacrifices

There is no denying that sacrifices will have to be made in order to build wealth. Unless you're starting out with millions in the bank and an unlimited supply of resources, there may be times when you have to forgo a splurge. If your goal is saving as much as possible, you may have to choose a staycation over that dream of spending two weeks in Fiji. You may have to forego charging something you really want to that credit card. Some would advise against using a credit card in the first place, and instead recommend using a charge card, for which the balance must be paid in full each month.

Making sacrifices in the short term in order to realize your financial goals in the long term doesn't mean you have to make a pledge of poverty, or totally deny yourself any pleasure or reward. It simply means that at times we may have to forgo some things we may really want in order to gain something more valuable in the long run. More value can be gained from investing that $100 per month than from biweekly visits to the hair salon. However, it is wonderful to treat ourselves to a salon visit every once in a while. The majority of the wealthy individuals with whom we spoke came from humble beginnings, and one common lesson that was taught to them early on was to live within one's means. Indeed, it was necessary for their survival. Although their present circumstances are vastly different and they can afford higher standards of living, they stressed these early lessons of being diligent in spending habits as crucial to their approach to wealth building.

Reuben fondly recalled that, although his family didn't have a lot, they had everything they needed, and his childhood was a happy one. Among the financial lessons he learned growing up is that a lot can be done with a little if one uses wisdom and makes good decisions. Not overspending was among the good decisions that enabled his grandmothers to contribute to the college education of several family members, even though his grandmothers didn't have a lot of money.

Managing Time and Prioritizing Values

Sometimes the sacrifice that's necessary is one of time rather than finances. This is the type of discipline that Brian argues is important if one is to achieve any goal in life. One of the main pieces of advice he gives to those whose goal is wealth accumulation is to first learn to manage their time. As he stated, "If you can't handle your time, you can't handle your money."

Brian's statement struck a nerve. It has taken us more than seven years to write this book. We had some very legitimate reasons for taking such a long time, among which were family, work, church, and social obligations. Although our daily lives look very different, we both have pressing responsibilities in all of these areas of our lives. Everyone, no matter what their life situation, has obligations that have a claim on their time and resources. We both have different life circumstances and different demands on our time, but we both respected the other's situation and validated each other's need to define what needed to get done and in what order. No person should be made to feel that his or her challenges or obligations are more or less important than another's. We all must decide for ourselves what our priorities are and how we're going to fulfill them. In other words, we each must run the race that's set before us. We are not called nor should we try to run someone else's race.

Early in the writing process, we worked with a coach who quickly pointed out things that could potentially be stumbling blocks and prevent us from sticking to our writing schedule. She gave us sage advice. We were slow to listen and have suffered the consequences. When talking through all the activities we were juggling and laying out the plan and timeline for getting things done, our coach advised that in order to be successful (i.e., have the book written and published according to the schedule we were proposing), we would have to let some of our activities go.

This was a hard pill to swallow. How could we say no to family obligations? What of the various organizations to which we had committed and were serving in a leadership capacity? How about that awesome mission opportunity for which everything just seemed to be lining up? Surely, we couldn't let that go! People all around us were depending on us. So being the superwomen that we considered ourselves to be, we proceeded as usual, with our plates full, and fully intending to write a book in a few months.

Needless to say, things didn't work out the way we thought they would. Somewhere along the line, we realized we simply had to make writing the book a priority and let some other things go, albeit temporarily. This meant some difficult but necessary conversations with family members about missing some activities and the shifting of responsibilities. Other times it meant taking some extra days off work to focus on writing. Sometimes we had to say no to hanging out with friends because we had a deadline to meet. None of these decisions were made lightly. They were all quite difficult to make. But they were also necessary in order to achieve our goal. This was our grind, physically and emotionally taxing, similar to the athletes above. These sacrifices we made were not forever, but they were short-term necessities for long-term goals.

Similarly, if wealth building is your long-term goal, some sacrifices will have to be made in the short term. Some difficult but necessary family conversations about forgoing certain purchases or attending costly events that are not within the budget will have to occur. At times, it may mean reading financial books or attending a seminar instead of streaming your favorite series for hours on end. The choice may not always be between lavish or modest spending. Sometimes, the financial outlay is for a worthy cause. However, we should always decide whether it is in line with our long-term goals.

From Sacrifice to Freedom

An important lesson we've learned (and are still trying to apply consistently) is that setting boundaries in time management, as well as in money management, is not just about sacrifice. Appropriately managing our time and money in accordance with our values and priorities ultimately leads to freedom and protects what matters most. Being clear on our values, and budgeting for them, also helps us make decisions free from guilt and worry. As we discussed in the previous chapter, to *Be Intentional* it's necessary to take stock of where you are from time to time and decide whether your current course of action is still the best one for the moment.

Let's return to the trip to Belize we introduced at the beginning of the chapter. Almost one year passed from the planning to the execution of that trip, and needless to say, our focus and energy was completely diverted from this book. Practically no writing took place during that time. In spite of that fact, we have no regrets about the experience because it was life-impacting for all those involved. Flying to Belize was the first airplane trip for some of these students. They learned about other cultures, and the ways of life of other people, and came away with a new appreciation for their own blessings. They were stretched beyond their comfort zones daily and rose to meet each new challenge in ways that surprised themselves. The trip, although a temporary detour from finishing our book, was completely in alignment with our values, and was worth the sacrifices that were made in order to make it happen. Along the same lines, we didn't say no to every social event in order to work on this book. Family time, self-care, and social connections are vital!

When working toward financial freedom, it may be necessary to change certain aspects of your plan as needs and opportunities arise. Once again, be open to the leading of the Holy Spirit in deciding which path to take. Sometimes money that was earmarked for savings may be needed to accomplish something else. At times like these we must allow ourselves grace to deviate from the plan and to get back to it as soon as it's feasible.

*Blessed are the diligent,
for they shall enjoy the fruits of their labor.*

To *Be Diligent* is to live in such a way that recognizes the importance of the sustained, consistent, hard work required to build wealth. It means refusing the prevailing instant-gratification tendency of society and refusing to take shortcuts that will comprise our success in the long run.

BE PRAYERFUL

God, please help me embrace and practice consistent effort toward my goals. May I remember what my values are; may I recognize that by seeking the education and assistance I need and establishing smart money habits around budgets, saving, and time management, I am actively reaffirming my values and fueling my ability to achieve freedom. Help me not be intimidated by any aspect of the financial journey. Strengthen my resolve to avoid debt and to live within my means. Amen.

BE DOERS

1. Commit to the process of wealth building and avoid get-rich-quick schemes.

2. Decide whether you need to enroll in a course, hire a financial planner, or utilize other educational resources.

3. Make sure your time and money are being spent in ways that are consistent with your goals and values.

Chapter 7

BE GENEROUS

Blessed are the generous,
for they shall prosper.

Sometime in the future, the last nail will be driven into Belize's newest Charity Medical Center. Perhaps right around the same time, Grenadians in an underserved part of the island will gather for the ribbon cutting of a state-of-the-art Library and Youth Innovation Center. Both of these projects will have been fully funded because two childhood friends from these same communities dared to follow the Spirit's prompting, and He blessed the work of their hands. The above scenario is aspirational for now. It's a peek into our dreams, and among the main reasons we began this journey of financial education and wealth building.

In the introduction to this book, we shared we have big dreams that require a lot of money. Everywhere we turn we see people in need and causes that tug at our heartstrings and drive us to our knees. We believe prayer is a powerful tool for change. But we also know the poor and marginalized need more than prayer. They need jobs, training, medical attention, and their basic needs of food, shelter, and clothing to be met. We desire to be part of the solution. We want to change lives, alleviate suffering, and open new pathways to prosperity for communities on the margins, including those that have nurtured us, on a scale far above what we can personally afford at the present time. We also want to leave a legacy of good stewardship and outrageous generosity for our children and loved ones to follow.

Our next *Be Attitude, Be Generous*, is a commitment to use, or to continue to use, our own personal wealth to benefit the lives of others. This *Be Attitude* calls us to be cheerful and empathetic givers, who choose to make a difference in the lives of our fellow brothers and sisters without seeking payback or reward. While the Bible is clear that when you give, others will give back to you, this is not our motivation for being generous. In other words, the goal of generosity should not be to add to our bank account or our bottom line. We don't give to others to get something in return. We give out of love. To *Be Generous* is an intentional de-centering of ourselves, our desires, our wants, and at times, even our needs, so we can see and respond to the needs of others. To *Be Generous* is a humbling acknowledgment that we are connected to each other as humans and a central tenet of our faith is our collective responsibility to love and care for each other.

It's important to note that *Be Generous* is separate from tithing. We believe generosity goes beyond the tithe. Tithing, as we discussed earlier, is the act of returning to God, the rightful owner, a tenth of what He has blessed us with. *Be Generous*, therefore, concerns what we do with the remaining ninety percent of our earnings after the tithe is paid.

A GENEROUS FATHER SHOULD
HAVE GENEROUS CHILDREN

Our first *Be Attitude, Be Right-Minded,* highlighted a critical mind-set we must embrace in order to have a healthy relationship with money. Namely, God is the generous owner of all the world's riches. He shows His generosity in many ways and to all people. He can't help Himself; it's just His nature. The ultimate act of God's generosity is, of course, the gift of His Son Jesus, but as we also discussed in the first chapter, He made us stewards over His creation, including riches. Generosity should therefore be a family trait among believers.

The ability to bless others or contribute to a particular cause that benefits society as a whole should be a joyful expression of who we are as God's children. It should be a natural outpouring of our identity, not something we're forced to do. Generally, as natural parents, we are pleased to see a positive family trait in our children that has been passed down from generation to generation. We sometimes proudly proclaim, "We [insert your family name here] are known for being athletic or artistic or [insert your particular gifting or trait]!" We can see a father or mother swell with pride as someone points out a good quality in their child, and attributes it to that parent. The same is true about our heavenly Father. He is proud as we, His children, are generous to others. More than that, He is glorified. We all can glorify our Father through this beautiful expression of who He is.

This type of generosity was exhibited by the children of Israel as they contributed gold, jewels, and other riches for the building of the first tabernacle in the wilderness in Exodus 35, by the women who supported Jesus's ministry in Luke 8, and by the widow with the two mites in Luke 21. The selflessness of the latter impressed the Lord Himself, who noted others gave out of their abundance while she gave sacrificially out of her lack. This generosity is exhibited today by those who give relief aid to victims of various disasters in the United States and around the world, who provide scholarships to students whose families aren't able to afford the rising costs of a college education, and by those who spend countless hours volunteering with various organizations.

Every day, and in so many ways, many people of all income levels, including those of humble means, show remarkable generosity, and impact the lives of others. Buying groceries for a family in need, giving gas money or transportation fare to someone so they can get to work, or donating items to charity are ways anyone can demonstrate generosity in everyday life. We don't need to go searching for examples of this fact. We've seen and experienced generosity throughout our entire lives. Among our family and friends, in our churches and communities, and even from strangers we've encountered along the way, there have been remarkable examples of openhandedness. While we're talking about our beliefs and obligation as Christians, generosity is by no means limited to Christianity. It is a human trait. But how much more so should we, who aspire to be Christlike, demonstrate this characteristic?

GENEROSITY IS A BIBLICAL MANDATE

Even if we don't intrinsically recognize the need to look and act like our Father in the area of generosity, we are commanded to do so. Charitable giving is one of the cornerstones of Christianity. There are many lessons about giving to others in the Bible. According to the instructions God gave the Israelites through Moses, they were to refrain from harvesting the grain from the edges of their fields and picking all the grapes from their vineyards. These provisions were for the poor and foreigners among them. The apostle Paul tells us in 1 Timothy that the rich should use their money to do good and be generous to those in need.

This attitude of selfless giving was evident in the wealthy Christians we interviewed. Much like tithing, many of them expressed their commitment to generosity without direct questioning from us. They embraced greater expressions of generosity as a natural outgrowth of reaching higher levels of financial success. Wayne, a best-selling author and media personality, spoke at length about his belief that he was given wealth so he could be an agent for change. Reuben, a former *Fortune* 500 executive agreed and shared his take on being generous: "It's really important to give back. If you have been blessed, then I believe, personally, that I was blessed in order to bless other people and projects that are in need."

God takes giving to the poor personally. He looks at it like a personal favor to Himself. Consider Proverbs 19:17, which says, "He who has pity on the poor lends to the Lord, and he will pay back what he has given." Consider also, the parable in Matthew 25:34–40, in which Jesus tells of those who will be blessed because they fed the hungry, gave water to the thirsty, welcomed strangers into their homes, clothed the naked, cared for the sick, and visited those in prison. He likens these acts of generosity as being done to Himself. As He said, "inasmuch as you did it to one of the least of these My brethren, you did it to Me" (v. 40). That's taking it personally! Whether we are called to be a "change agent" or "blessed to be a blessing," the importance of being generous cannot be overstated. Whatever our level of income, it's clear God entrusted His resources to us so we can in turn bless others. This practice should only increase as we build wealth.

GENEROSITY BENEFITS
BOTH GIVER AND RECIPIENT

The benefits gained by those on the receiving end of others' generosity are obvious. Among them are financial assistance, a listening ear when one is sorely needed, or help with performing daily tasks. What about the giver? Does she benefit in any way, or did she just lose money, time, and energy? We suggest to you that the giver absolutely benefits. Many of us can recall that feeling of satisfaction we get when we do something good for someone else. This is known as a "warm glow." As it turns out, these are more than just temporary good feelings.

Increasingly, studies have shown the benefits of generosity are far-reaching and are both physical and mental in nature. They include stress reduction, supporting our physical health, enhancing our sense of purpose, fighting depression, and increasing our lifespan. One study shows that gift-giving activates pathways in the brain that release oxytocin, one of the four so-called feel-good hormones. In short, the more generous people are, the happier they are. Those are some pretty powerful benefits! Isn't it just like God to ask us to do something and reward us exponentially for being obedient?

In addition, generosity tends to be contagious. Fania recalls attending a fundraiser for an organization that provides tuition and other forms of assistance to unwed mothers who have matriculated at colleges and universities, where she was bowled over by the boisterous atmosphere brought on by donations. It became a party-like atmosphere as individuals made pledges and were cheered on and joined by others who wanted to meet or exceed those pledges.

Perhaps this phenomenon is partly responsible for the behavior of the children of Israel in the building of the temple that we mentioned

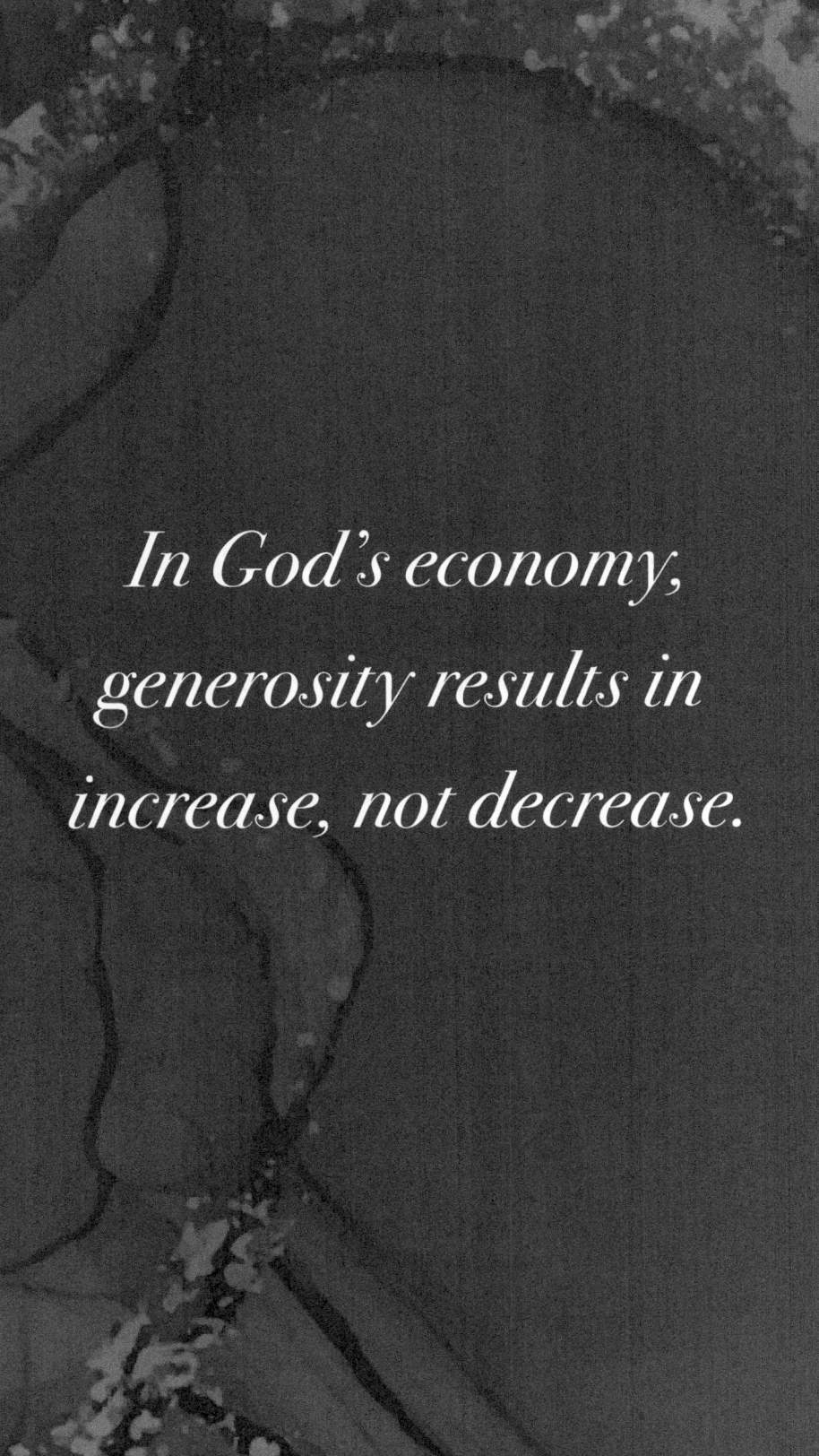

In God's economy, generosity results in increase, not decrease.

earlier. As each individual and tribe witnessed their neighbors giving generously to the Lord, they were spurred on to do the same. King David understood this well. He declared his devotion to God by giving of his personal treasure toward the building of the temple in Jerusalem. We see in 1 Chronicles 29 that, after this, the leaders of the people gave freely and wholeheartedly to the work of the temple.

We could say the effects of being generous are counterintuitive, in the sense that giving something away results in a net increase to the giver. A generous person will prosper. Whoever refreshes others will be refreshed (see Proverbs 11:25). Getting something in return should not be our motivation for giving, but it is a biblically ordained result. Luke 6:38 tells us, "Give, and it will be given to you: good measure, pressed down, shaken together, and running over, will be put into your bosom. For with the same measure that you use, it will be measured to you." In God's economy, generosity results in increase, not decrease. It is indeed better to give than to receive.

IT'S NOT JUST ABOUT MONEY

Generosity isn't solely about money. Liberality in giving includes showing love, care, and compassion. Some of the ways we demonstrate these things are by sharing our knowledge with others, lending a helping hand to someone, or just listening. We've all benefited or, at some point in our lives, will benefit, from the generosity of others. Therefore, we should be only too glad for the opportunity to bless someone else. We mentioned earlier that we have similar stories of immigrant mothers who exemplified hard work and self-sacrifice. Another very interesting similarity is the generosity that both they and we received at the hands of some of their employers. Both of our mothers worked as so-called domestics for various middle-class White families in New York City and the suburbs of New Jersey. Many of these employers went above and beyond what was expected in both their treatment of our parents and in exposing us to resources and ideas we would otherwise never have.

They allowed us to be present as our moms took care of their homes and families, allowed us to use their extensive libraries to satisfy our curious minds, recommended us for summer employment at their prestigious firms, and gave generously to various fundraising endeavors in which we were involved throughout the years. Many years after our mothers' employment with these families have ended, we remember these individuals whose kindness and generosity impacted our lives in lasting ways. Other blessings in our educational journey— scholarships, internships, fellowships, travel grants and the like—were funded by generous individuals. Blessed to be a blessing isn't a theoretical exercise for us. We are living it each day. Think about your own life. Who are the people who have impacted you?

One of the truly amazing lessons we learned throughout the process of writing this book is that people are more generous than we think. There are those who are waiting for the opportunity to share their talents, and often the only way we'll tap into these resources is to ask. The prospect of reaching out to individuals, the majority of whom were perfect strangers, and asking them to share their stories, was daunting to say the least. Their willingness to give their time and to share anecdotes about their journey (not all of which were positive), and their overall generosity of spirit truly astounded us. Not only were these individuals willing to speak with us, but they were also willing to point us in the direction of others with whom we wished to speak. These are busy individuals, with myriad responsibilities, and yet they took the time to help strangers. They received nothing in return. We couldn't afford their services anyway. They were indeed living out the principles of which they spoke.

David, the accomplished leadership expert and successful CEO, shared his philosophy about the responsibility to share knowledge with others: "There were people who were placed in my life that were a total blessing that sowed into me. And I had to make sure I was humble enough to receive that information... And then when I had that information ... not to be so selfish not to share it with others. And I think those are faith principles in action. I think if you sow good seed, you can get a harvest. So, then that means I don't want to hoard my seed and not help young businesspeople that are coming up in this generation."

We all find ourselves in need of help sometimes. Are we also willing to lend a helping hand to others? There's a lot we can do right now, with what we have. We don't have to wait until we have a lot of money to make a difference. Things like answering a question, sharing a tip, or providing advice may not seem like a big deal but could go a long way in helping someone else on their path. You can be a mentor at every stage of your career and in every phase of your business development. There's always someone with whom you can share, even if it's only lessons learned or best practices.

DRAWING A LINE

Is there such a thing as giving too much? After everything we've said above, isn't the answer a resounding no? After all, aren't we supposed to give until it hurts? Where does being generous end and being used begin? These are important considerations because unfortunately there are some people who are only too willing to be on the receiving end of others' generosity and will abuse the situation. In addition, we need to do heart checks here as well. Giving to others, like anything else, can become an idol in our lives. What motivates our giving? Are we doing it out of guilt, to get the applause or approval of others, or to prove how noble we are? Sometimes our well-meaning tendency to share and care for others is driven by guilt, unrealistic expectations, or practices that stem from unhealthy, co-dependent relationships. As in all things, our giving should be Spirit-led and will therefore be for the right reasons.

By virtue of necessity and tradition, people of the African diaspora are highly communal, generous, and community minded. The needs of our community are pronounced and many of our families depend on our willingness to share to make ends meet. Like many other immigrants from across the diaspora, our families routinely send money and goods to help offset the needs of loved ones still living in our home countries.

One of our shared experiences is receiving barrels sent by our mothers after they immigrated to the United States. The excitement of receiving a container filled with food, clothing, and other necessities, handpicked by a loved one, was palpable for the entire household. As children, we were especially eager for the carefully wrapped toys, books, and special treats bound up in tins that, when emptied, would be put to further good use for baking and storage. We felt the love of our mothers through these barrels and knew we were not forgotten.

Years later, we joined our mothers in doing the sending. We now understand the pressure to master the engineering feat of filling the barrel with three times more than it was designed to hold and getting it to stay closed. (Hint: the key is to get someone else to add their weight on top of the lid to further compress the contents while you firmly affix the lock in place!)

These memories, along with others of family members or even neighbors coming together in support of each other, are some of the fondest from our childhoods. It's a privilege to have the means and the opportunity to give, whether in support of family members in a different country, a neighbor down the block, or a community member in need. Unfortunately, we've also suffered the consequences of hastily made, ill-informed decisions to give away the little one has, thereby leaving the household at a deficit—of liquidating savings accounts or not saving at all in order to meet family obligations, or to respond to frequent calls for help.

Many of these decisions were made based on unrealistic family expectations, guilt, or a misunderstanding of Scripture and what God expects, as we respond to those in need. On the one hand is the desire to be generous, while on the other is the obligation to take care of our own households. We must strike a balance. The biblical call to charity is not a call to indiscriminate, self-defeating giving. Neither is it a call to perpetuate a culture of dependency on others. This may sound strange, but at some point, giving can become detrimental to both parties involved.

Our generosity must be governed by wisdom and a correct understanding of how God is leading us to respond. Not every financial need can be solved with a financial answer. Sometimes the responsibility of responding to a need is not ours or ours alone. It could be that the person would be better served with help finding employment, thereby fostering a long-term solution to their financial woes. Maybe they need resources that teach how to better manage what they already have. Unfettered giving, without following the leading of the Spirit, may end up having a detrimental effect on all parties. Making financial decisions based on guilt or any improper motive will undermine our progress in building wealth and prevent us from being in a position to truly help our families and communities.

BE GENEROUS WITH YOURSELF

After the advice about having the proper perspective, taking risks, working hard, and blessing others, came the reminder to be good to ourselves. Once again, this generosity applies to both finances and other resources. There's a blessing in enjoying the fruits of your labor. The satisfaction and pride that comes from working hard and providing well for yourself or your family are unparalleled.

We'd be wise to heed the advice of King Solomon who said, "It is good and fitting for one to eat and drink, and to enjoy the good of all his labor in which he toils under the sun all the days of his life which God gives him; for it is his heritage. As for every man to whom God has given riches and wealth, and given him power to eat of it, to receive his heritage and rejoice in his labor—this is the gift of God" (Ecclesiastes 5:18–19). The life we are blessed with is a gift from God. Any wealth or riches we attain are also blessings from Him. Therefore, we can and should joyfully receive and enjoy all of God's blessings.

It took some time for Anna, co-owner of an engineering company, to learn this lesson. She admits she spent years of forgoing vacations and not doing anything if it meant she could save money. She credits her husband with being a wonderful influence to help her, as she described it, "learn to live a little." Over time, she learned how to establish boundaries so she could treat herself and enjoy the results of her hard work. Taking a vacation, a trip to the spa, or purchasing nice things for ourselves should not leave us racked with guilt. As we described earlier, we're not called to give away every cent we earn. After putting everything in its proper place, in alignment with the order set by the Lord, we can and should enjoy the financial gains we've made. It's wise to do periodic heart checks to make sure our motivations for making particular purchases are the right ones.

In considering purchases and other lifestyle decisions, Pastor Malcolm, the well-regarded pastor and successful entrepreneur, asks himself questions like, "Is this covering up for insecurity? Is this me trying to be the cool kid at the table because I wasn't when I was in the seventh grade? Is this just wanton materialism? These questions reveal broken areas in our lives that need to be addressed, because if they're not, we often turn to idols to fill the gaping holes they leave." As we stated in *Be Spirit-Led*, this doesn't have to be our path. With our priorities in place and our heart fully aligned with the will of God, we can indeed enjoy the material blessings and bounty He provided.

Blessed are the generous,
for they shall prosper.

Be Generous, as described in this chapter, is an invitation to see and respond to the needs of others. Not for riches or rewards, but because we are called to exemplify generosity, which is a defining attribute of our heavenly Father. Our generosity is not limited solely to money. We can be a blessing with our time and other resources. We are encouraged to establish healthy boundaries around our giving, and to avoid unwise decisions based on guilt. Finally, we are encouraged to extend generosity to ourselves, as guided by the Spirit, so we can enjoy the fruits of our labor.

BE PRAYERFUL

Father, I want to be generous like You. Please help me show Your love to others by being a liberal and joyful giver. Help me be wise in determining what causes to support, yet always willing to follow your leading and prompting in every situation. Help me find joy in giving to others and enjoying the result of my labor. May I see both as gifts from You. Amen.

BE DOERS

1. What resources do I possess right now that I can use to bless others?

2. Where do I need to exercise greater wisdom in my giving?

3. How can I have guilt-free enjoyment of what God has blessed me with?

CONCLUSION

When we asked God how we could get rich without going spiritually broke, we had no idea He would answer immediately and specifically by leading us to thoughtful and inspiring individuals who would bless us with their wisdom and insight. Wealth building was central to our discussions, but it wasn't the whole. Our talks pressed us to look inwardly at our habits of mind and the state of our spiritual life. We neither anticipated nor at times enjoyed this journey of self-reflection. But it was necessary, and we are profoundly changed. Through this process, we were able to see God's faithfulness more clearly throughout our lives—how He has provided for us and equipped us. How He orchestrated divine opportunities, forged connections, and ultimately stirred our hearts, to achieve great things for His glory. The seven *Be Attitudes* summarized next have become our blueprint for not only wealth building but living in our legacy.

1. BE RIGHT-MINDED

Approach wealth building with the right mindset. Know that God is the generous creator and owner of all things, and you are His beloved, who is worthy to receive His financial blessings, and capable of multiplying what He has given.

2. BE A GOOD STEWARD

Commit to stewarding God's money and resources with care and integrity. Demonstrate your trust in, and have obedience to, Him, by making tithing a cornerstone of your stewardship.

3. BE SPIRIT-LED

Establish a Spirit-led lifestyle, by getting to know Him, through studying His Word, and cultivating a rich prayer life. Turn to Him first for guidance on all decisions, financial or otherwise. Invite the Spirit to continuously check your heart so your attitude and financial priorities remain aligned with His will.

4. BE BOLD

Take risks. Be confident and courageous. Don't let fear hold you back from setting ambitious goals, taking action, and shining brilliantly.

5. BE INTENTIONAL

Take personal responsibility for your own financial success by clarifying your goals, creating informed and realistic plans for success, and adjusting as necessary.

6. BE DILIGENT

Put in the work. Learn and implement core financial fundamentals to increase your assets, avoid debt, save, and invest. Refuse to take shortcuts that will compromise your success.

7. BE GENEROUS

Freely give to causes and individuals in need. Establish healthy boundaries to avoid unwise financial decisions. Extend generosity to yourself—enjoy the hard-earned fruits of your labor.

In the past we thought of legacy as the realization of a finished work. From this perspective, we would plant the seeds of legacy while living, but the harvest or fruit would only truly be realized after we depart this life. Legacy seemed far off, not capable of being seen or enjoyed while we are still alive. The culmination of a life well lived. These last few years have shown us that legacy is much closer at hand. Of course, some seeds may not be fully realized in our lifetime, but we are convinced that our impact can and should be felt, even while we're alive. Material wealth is the least permanent part of our legacy. Markets can crash, fortunes reverse in an instant, and indeed, rust and moth do decay, as the Scripture warns.

As you know by now, we believe building generational wealth and setting the example of God-glorifying financial stewardship are important aspects of leaving a legacy. However, we urge you not to miss the greater goal of leaving a true legacy that cannot be measured in dollars and cents. We must live more fully and richly in Christ, while alive, to reap the benefits ourselves, and point others to an eternal legacy. This is ultimately why we have written this book. We hope through our work your finances will increase and your soul will abound.

SCRIPTURE INDEX

GENESIS

1:1 26
1:26-28 26
1:27 31
14:18-20 42

EXODUS

4:2 58
35 127

LEVITICUS

27:30 43

DEUTERONOMY

8:18 . . . . . .9, 28, 31

I SAMUEL

3:5 60
3:1 60
3:7 60

I CHRONICLES

29 132

PSALMS

24:1 24
65:11 47
145:9 32

PROVERBS

1:5 117
3:5-6 59
3:9 43
10:4 112
11:14 117
11:25 132
13:11 52
15:22 117
19:17 129
22:7 50
22:29 83

ECCLESIASTES

5:18-19 137

HABAKKUK

2:2 102

MALACHI

3:8-9 43
3:10 . . . . . . 44, 55
3:11 46

MATTHEW

5 . . . . .15, 16
5:45 32
7:11 . . . . .31, 27
19:16 34
19:21 35
23:23 43
25:14-30 26
25:26 47
25:34-40 129

LUKE

6:38 132
8 127
14:28-30 102
21 127

ROMANS

8:14 59
8:37 83

I CORINTHIANS

4:2 42

II CORINTHIANS

9:8 47

EPHESIANS

2:10 83
6:17 83

PHILIPPIANS

2:3 86
4:13 83

I TIMOTHY

6:10 . . . . 13, 34

HEBREWS

7:1-10 43
11 38

JAMES

1:5 83
1:17 27

NOTES

1. "Ariel-Schwab Black Investor Survey (2022)," Schwab Moneywise, Charles Schwab, accessed April 22, 2024, https://www.schwabmoneywise.com/tools-resources/ariel-schwab-survey-2022.

2. DeForest B. Soaries, Jr., *dfree: Breaking Free from Financial Slavery* (Grand Rapids: Zondervan, 2011), 17.

3. Charles R. Swindoll, *The Mystery of God's Will* (Thomas nelson Publishing, 1999), 30.

4. Pete Grieg, *How to Pray: A Simple Guide for Normal People* (NavPress, 2019), xviii.

5. Ibid, xviii.

6. Ibid, xviii.

7. "Bold." Merriam-Webster.com Dictionary, Merriam-Webster, https://www.merriam-webster.com/dictionary/bold. Accessed 22 Apr. 2024.

8. Kathy Kay and Claire Chipman, *The Confidence Code: The Science and Art of Self-Assurance— What Women Should Know* (Harper Business, 2014).

9. James Clear, *Atomic Habits: An Easy and Proven Way to Build Good Habits and Break Bad Ones* (Penguin Random House, 2018), 38.

10. "The Thing about Goals," Seth's Blog, accessed on April 22, 2024, https://seths.blog/2009/01/the-thing-about/#:~:text=If%20you%20don't%20have%20a%20goal%20you%20don't,fun%2C%20in%20the%20short%20run.

11. "Neuroscience Explains Why You Need to Write Down Your Goals If You Actually Want to Achieve Them," *Forbes*, April 15, 2018, https://www.forbes.com/sites/markmurphy/2018/04/15/neuroscience-explains-why-you-need-to-write-down-your-goals-if-you-actually-want-to-achieve-them/?sh=1fdcf6e79059.

12. "The Power of Writing Down Your Goals: Evidence from Multiple Studies," Oak Journal, February 8, 2023, https://oakjournal.com/blogs/resources/the-power-of-writing-down-your-goals-evidence-from-multiple-studies#:~:text=The%20first%20study%20that%20we,than%20those%20who%20did%20not.

Acknowledgments

Thank You:

To the individuals we interviewed, who shared their time, personal stories, and wisdom with us.

To those who connected us to these generous individuals.

To those who read drafts of the book in many different stages, providing us with helpful feedback and sage advice.

To our friends and church family, for your support and prayers.

To our families, who encouraged, sacrificed, and loved us through these long years of writing.

We are forever grateful.

About the Authors

Cassandra C. Lewis, PhD is grateful for her life that blends a passion for education, commitment to family and culture, together with a love of laughter, good food, and world travel. She lives in Maryland with husband Essentino and three children.

Fania Denton lives in New York City and loves music, museums, and the outdoors. She's always been drawn to the turquoise waters and sun-kissed shores of her homeland, Belize, and her ultimate dream is to set sail across the Caribbean Sea.

www.ingramcontent.com/pod-product-compliance
Lightning Source LLC
Chambersburg PA
CBHW061804120626

46550CB00005B/2137